OXFORD READINGS IN PHILOSOPHY
Series Editor G. J. Warnock

THE PHILOSOPHY OF PERCEPTION

THE PHILOSOPHY OF PERCEPTION

Edited by
G. J. WARNOCK

OXFORD UNIVERSITY PRESS
1967

Oxford University Press, Ely House, London W.1

GLASGOW   NEW YORK   TORONTO   MELBOURNE   WELLINGTON
CAPE TOWN   SALISBURY   IBADAN   NAIROBI   LUSAKA   ADDIS ABABA
BOMBAY   CALCUTTA   MADRAS   KARACHI   LAHORE   DACCA
KUALA LUMPUR   HONG KONG   TOKYO

FILMSET BY ST PAUL'S PRESS, MALTA
PRINTED IN GREAT BRITAIN
AT THE UNIVERSITY PRESS, OXFORD
BY VIVIAN RIDLER
PRINTER TO THE UNIVERSITY

CONTENTS

INTRODUCTION

IN AT LEAST one respect, a collection of recent or contemporary articles on perception would have been easier to make some twenty or more years ago than it is today. There would have been more to choose from; and for a start we may ask—guessing a little, as must be admitted—why this should be so.

From the time of Descartes until very recent years, there had been in the field, and never far from the centre of philosophical attention, a variety of competing theories of perception; this was not, any more than any other, a region in which philosophers were in general and equable agreement. Nevertheless, though the doctrines espoused by philosophers might differ, there were certain general presuppositions to which all or practically all, often tacitly, subscribed; and these seemed to pose, and to pose with reasonable clarity, the main problem that the differing doctrines were intended to solve. First, it was generally supposed, even taken for granted, that human knowledge in general had a stratified or layer-like character—that at least it had and must have *foundations*, and hence that it was plainly the business of the philosopher to identify and narrowly scrutinize these foundations, and then to show how, and how much of, what passes for knowledge was or could be securely supported upon them. It was of course further supposed by most, though not indeed by all, that perception, the exercise of the human senses, at least contributed largely to knowledge, and not only largely but also fundamentally. But second, it was also almost universally supposed that perception, like knowledge itself, was a stratified affair—that here too there was (must be) a basis, a species of data, and distinct from this those inferences, constructions, interpretations which are expressed in the relatively high-level judgments of perception of everyday life.

Thus to most philosophers, for some centuries, at least the *problems* seemed quite clear. Let it be agreed that perception figures largely, and fundamentally, in the acquisition of knowledge; what then are the questions that arise about perception? It seemed quite clear that the questions must be: first, what are the data? and second, how do we build upon them? What is the nature of those entities of which, in perceiving, we are basically, directly, immediately aware?

1

How is this immediate awareness itself to be characterized? And then it must be considered by what process, by what kind of inference or construction or interpretation, we pass from awareness of data to our ordinary, but complex, perceptual awareness of and judgments about the world and its contents. It was argued, at a late stage of the philosophers' debates on these matters, that the issues were not ontological, but logical or linguistic—it was not a question of two kinds of *things*, sense-data and material objects, and of the relation between them, but of two kinds of *language*, sense-datum language and material-object language, and of the relation between these.[1] But this latter-day contribution, while it altered the ostensible aim, appeared not greatly to change the form of the traditional and familiar issues. These appeared to survive, more fashionably dressed.

I think it can be said that today the whole position is less clear— or rather, that what once *seemed* very clear no longer seems so. A few years ago Professor Ryle remarked to me that 'the philosophy of perception isn't only in the melting-pot—it's in it upside down'; and by this pregnant saying I take him to have meant that philosophers have not only come to distrust the terms in which, by long tradition, philosophical problems about perception have been posed and dis- cussed: they are also not yet by any means sure how those problems might be posed and discussed more profitably. Perhaps they are not even quite sure what the 'problems' are.

Professor Bouwsma's paper, the first in the present collection and much the earliest in date, excellently illustrates one crucial respect in which old certitudes have dissolved. It had been, since the time of Descartes, a central tenet of all philosophical theories of percep- tion that ordinary objects and states of affairs in the world are not themselves perceptual data; they, and their properties and states and doings, are not, in perception, 'given'. There is always something *else* that is 'given'; and it is precisely their relation to this 'given' which constitutes the problem. Thus G. E. Moore, in considering the nature of vision, has no doubt at all that seeing, say, a hand involves, and indeed is based in some way upon, some more direct awareness or apprehension of something else; and accordingly for him the philo- sopher's problem is, having identified this something else, to show how it functions as an element in seeing a hand.[2] Moore indeed,

---

[1] See, e.g., A. J. Ayer's *Foundations of Empirical Knowledge*, pp. 46–57; and J. L. Austin's comments in *Sense and Sensibilia*, pp. 55–61 (See Bibliography for all publications whose details are not given in the footnotes to this Introduction.)

[2] See, e.g., Moore's *Some Main Problems of Philosophy* (Allen and Unwin, London, 1953), chapter 2. This work was written more than forty years before its date of publication.

characteristically, is very far from supposing that this preliminary task of identification is easy; but Bouwsma argues that, for all the pains that he takes, his attempt to direct his readers' attention to the kind of datum-entity he wishes to talk about is a total failure. And this raises the question: is it really there at all? Moore assumes that there *must* be something of the kind he is looking for; but may this conviction, Bouwsma asks, be itself an illusion? When I hear a car, there is indeed, besides the car itself, a sound that I hear; but when I look at my hand, what is there to be seen that is not, simply, my hand? Perhaps seeing is in this respect simply different from hearing. But if so, it seems no longer possible even to state what had been supposed to be *the* philosophical question about seeing.

The two linked papers by Professors Hirst and Wollheim discuss, in a quite different manner and more generally, what is in a way the same fundamental issue. Is it really the case—as had long been tradition-ally supposed—that there is involved in all 'observing' of ordinary things some simpler, more basic 'sensing' of (presumably) simpler and more basic items? For if not, then *all* traditional theories are radically undermined, and the traditional problems cannot even be intelligibly stated. Professor Hirst does not take, though he mentions, the drastic course of declaring 'sensing' to be 'a myth', but it is con-spicuous nonetheless how defensive his account of it is; and Professor Wollheim, besides questioning whether any distinction between observing and 'sensing' could be either simple, or exhaustive, or final, questions also the fundamental traditional view that, whatever sensing and what is sensed may be, at least we are *more certain* about what is sensed than about anything that is observed, and hence that sensing must have priority in the hierarchy of knowledge.[1] Mr. Quinton's paper is the most wide-ranging of all, but once again is principally concerned to argue that traditional problems about perception have been misconceived—that is, that the very statement of the problems, before any 'solutions' are offered, involves the employment of notions, such as that of 'direct awareness', which have not been and probably cannot be made unambiguously intellig-ible. There is no question, then, of going on in the same old way. Statements *about* experience, Quinton suggests, do not constitute in any sense the logical foundation of all beliefs and judgments about the material world; and while doubtless experience *itself* could be said to be the foundation of most knowledge and belief, the question of exactly how this is so is not logical but empirical—a

[1] On this point see also Austin's *Sense and Sensibilia*, particularly Section X.

question, in that case, for psychologists and not for philosophers.

A different line of thought, for the adequate illustration of which no space could be found in this collection, should be mentioned here. Many writers, from Locke in the seventeenth century to H. A. Prichard in the twentieth, have supposed that the philosopher's business with perception, at any rate in part, is to correct the errors of the un-instructed plain man. Reflection on the phenomena of perceptual illusion, or on the causal transactions and processes involved in perceiving, or both, were often taken to establish that the plain man's beliefs are in certain ways mistaken—Prichard, for example, put for-ward the somewhat drastic opinion that, at least in the case of vision, ordinary judgments are *always* mistaken through misidentification of what is actually perceived. A latter-day amendment substantially modified this thesis; it was maintained, conspicuously by Professor Ayer, that the traditional arguments revealed, not error in ordinary beliefs, but at most inadequacies in ordinary language, and according-ly required the production, not of correct philosophical doctrines, but rather of a specially-tailored philosophical terminology. Still, in one form or another the opinion was at one time widely held that the philosopher somehow could and should effect improvements upon what, without his aid, would ordinarily be either believed or said. But here too old certitudes have been subject to much erosion. It has been argued, most powerfully by J. L. Austin in the post-humously published *Sense and Sensibilia*, that the venerable 'argument from illusion' is itself a tangle of 'sophistry and illusion', depending partly upon misrepresentation of the nature of the phenomena called (often mis-called) illusions, and partly upon attribution to the plain man of queer and vulnerable ideas which in fact there is no good reason to suppose that he holds. Rather similarly, Austin argues that the notion that there is need for an invented philosophical terminol-ogy—the terminology of 'sense-data'—is supported, so far as it is seriously supported at all, by arguments which involve neglecting the very various and often subtle resources of existing, quite ordinary language. What *are* the mistakes the plain man is supposed to make? Alternatively, where *is* it that the ordinary speaker is supposed to run into terminological difficulties? Until these questions are, if they can be, adequately answered, it cannot be clear what the philosopher, on these lines, can take himself to be doing, or indeed that there is need for him to do anything at all.

The notion that reflection on the causal processes of perceiving may reveal inadequacies in 'common-sense' ideas has been less exhaustively examined, and is certainly not yet dead. Professor Hirst, for example, has argued this case in a recent book[1]—though he does not, to my mind, show at all convincingly that 'common-sense' does embrace the views which he thinks can be refuted by philosophical reflection. But this leads us on to another matter. Supposing it to be true (as can scarcely be denied) that perceiving is at least in part a causal transaction, how exactly should this truth be brought into the account? The 'causal theory' of perception has been for centuries one of the leading contenders in the field; can it still be intelligibly stated, or has it too fallen victim to the collapse of traditional landmarks? This is the question to which Mr. Grice addresses himself in his exceedingly ingenious and resourceful contribution to his symposium with Professor White; and it will be observed that, although he holds as against many others that the notion of 'sense-data', or at least of 'sense-datum statements', *can* be intelligibly introduced, he is as far as possible from supposing that that enterprise is wholly plain sailing. Nor does he claim that he has shown the 'causal theory' to be true; its truth, he thinks, in the sense he explains, is 'not out of the question'.

The paper in this collection by Professor Sibley is of a very different and in a sense a less melancholy kind. It would be indeed misleading and unfair to say of the other papers that they are, in effect, predominantly negative; for one thing, it is a positive service to correct philosophical error, nor, as a rule, can this effectively be done without some considerable deployment of philosophical truth. Still, it seems undeniable that many of these papers exist, as does a very great deal of recent philosophical writing on perception, as it were in the backwash of rejected and receding theories. The old confidence in a hierarchical structure of knowledge has faded; the old trust in a simple, though indeed problematic, dichotomy between 'ideas' and objects, 'sense-data' and material things, the 'given' and the constructed or inferred, 'experience' and its objects, has been sadly shaken. Thus it has come to seem no longer profitable, or even possible, actively to debate the merits of those large-scale theories that were founded upon trust in those presuppositions, and philosophers have inevitably been much concerned merely with arguing that, and why, this is so. But of course this is not all that remains for philosophers to do; it is not simply a matter of burying the corpses after the battle is won, nor even of minutely scrutinizing the casualties in the hope of discerning some

---

[1] In his contribution to Wyburn, Pickford, and Hirst, *Human Senses and Perception*, for which see the Bibliography at the end of this volume.

flicker of recoverable life. For the vocabulary of perception, and the concepts wielded in the use of that vocabulary, remain; and of course these are not problematic *only* if first misrepresented in philosophical theory. On the contrary; one ill effect of traditional theories was that, if anything, they tended to conceal the extreme complexity of their subject-matter, to make the concepts of perception look more homogeneous, simpler, and tidier than they really are. For 'perception' is not after all, though it has often been treated as, some single, unitary phenomenon. We have, for a start, not one sense, but several senses; these differ widely among themselves, and also in their 'objects' and typical modes of exercise. We make, on the basis of employing one or more of our senses, judgments of immensely various kinds—varying with our capacities, with our aims or interests, with the circumstances of particular cases, with our expectations, with our state of hesitation or confidence, and in many other ways. Once we abandon the notion that there are, seriously to be considered, just *two* kinds of perceptual judgments, those about 'sense-data' and those about 'material things', we are free to take note of the fact that there are hugely *many* kinds, and to embark on the business of elucidating them and their interrelations. Professor Sibley undertakes, without theoretical preconceptions, an enquiry of this kind into the particular case of seeing; and there is clearly no shortage of subject-matter for similar enquiry into other cases.

I shall end by simply pointing out—not attempting to solve—one instructive problem that seems to me to arise out of Professor Bouwsma's paper. There is, he points out, no common noun associated with the verb 'see' in the way in which the common nouns 'sound', 'taste', 'smell' are familiarly associated with the verbs 'hear', 'taste', 'smell'. And this suggests the question: why not? Is this just a fact about the world—the fact that, when I look for something that, in seeing my hand, functions as the *sound* does when I hear a car, there is, straightforwardly, no such thing? Or is it perhaps a fact about my senses—the fact that the sense of sight differs in just this way, in human beings, from the sense of hearing? Or again, is it perhaps a mere accident of vocabulary that, in the vocabulary of vision, this billet has been left unoccupied? Or might it not rather be a conceptual truth that, our concept of an object being what it is, there is no room, as it were between the seer and the seen, for visual 'intermediaries' on the analogy of sounds and smells? Might these various suggestions be combined, or even found not to be independent of one another, and if so, how are they inter-related? Such questions as these, I think, point in at least one direction in which there are still plenty of problems for investigation. For even if we abandon the long-accepted idea that the problem is that of the relation between 'sense-data' and 'material things', it is still clear that there are connections, both important and unobvious, between what we know of and say about our environment and its contents, and the means and modes in which, in perception, we become aware of them. It is obvious that there must be close interdependence here. What we take the perceivable world to *be* must be some sort of function of the ways in which we are aware of it; and conversely, what perceiving is, or even could be, said to consist in cannot be independent of *what* is to be said to be perceived. There is not only, then, the task of finally dispelling what we may regard as the fogs and confusions of traditional theories. Nor is there only, in addition to that, the complex business of accurately delineating, and clearly distinguishing, the concepts that are actually wielded in judgments of perception. There is the task also of *understanding* this group or family of concepts—of explaining, not merely describing, its conspicuous features, of seeing whence they derive and what it is that derives from them. To this we may add also, as a problem still in need of much investigation, the question of determining the logical relations between those things which the plain man believes and says about the world as he observes it with the unaided senses and in ordinary circumstances, and those other things said, on very different grounds and with very different ends in view, by psychologists, physiologists, physicists, and others.[1] Even if it be true, as I believe it is, that philosophical interest in perception is at present rather in a state of suspended animation, it is certainly not true that this is to be explained by the want of problems. As old questions—some of them—fade away, new questions emerge.

[1] There is a lively discussion of this particular issue in G. Ryle, *Dilemmas*, chapter 5. See also J. J. C. Smart, *Philosophy and Scientific Realism* (Routledge, London, 1963).

I

MOORE'S THEORY OF SENSE-DATA

O. K. BOUWSMA

I

I WANT in this essay to discuss a few sentences from Professor
Moore's 'A Defence of Common Sense', published in the volume
containing the second series of contributions to *Contemporary British
Philosophy*. These sentences are contained in part IV of that contribution. In this part Professor Moore is expounding what he regards
as the correct analysis of such sentences as 'This is a hand', 'That is
the sun', 'This is a dog', etc. Involved in this exposition is the
assertion: 'whenever I know or judge such a proposition to be true,
there is always some sense-datum about which the proposition in
question is a proposition—some sense-datum which is a subject of
the proposition in question'.[1] Professor Moore goes on to recognize
'that some philosophers have . . . doubted whether there are any such
things as other philosophers have meant by "sense-data"',[2] and in
order to make sure that his readers may be persuaded, he goes on with
the following attempt at definition, which I quote.

Professor Moore writes:

And in order to point out to the reader what sort of things I mean by
sense-data, I need only ask him to look at his own right hand. If he does this
he will be able to pick out something (and unless he is seeing double, only
one thing) with regard to which he will see that it is, at first sight, a natural
view to take, that that thing is identical, not indeed, with his whole right hand,
but with that part of its surface which he is actually seeing, but will also (on

From *The Philosophy of G. E. Moore*, ed. P. A. Schillp, Vol. IV of the Library of Living
Philosophers (Northwestern University Press, Evanston, Ill., 1942), pp. 203-21.
(Future editions to be published by Open Court, La Salle, Ill. and by Cambridge
University Press, London.) Reprinted by permission of the Library of Living
Philosophers, Inc.

[1] *Contemporary British Philosophy*, Second Series, 217.
[2] Ibid., 217.

a little reflection) be able to see that it is doubtful whether it can be identical with the part of the surface of his hand in question. Things *of the sort* (in a certain respect) of which this thing is, which he sees in looking at his hand, and with regard to which he can understand how some philosophers should have supposed it to be the part of the surface of his hand which he is seeing, while others have supposed that it can't be, are what I mean by sense-data. I therefore define the term in such a way that it is an open question whether the sense-datum which I now see in looking at my hand and which is a sense-datum of my hand, is or is not identical with that part of its surface which I am now actually seeing.[1]

I propose first to discuss some difficulties in this paragraph. Professor Moore invites his readers to pick out something, but his directions for doing this are not clear. Commonly if one is asked to pick out something, the something is described. Out of this bowl, pick out the red flower; out of this sheaf pick out the longest straw. We should all know how to follow these directions. But Professor Moore's directions are not like this. Apparently you simply pick out something; that is, as you are looking at your hand, and keeping your eye on your hand, you pick out something. Suppose you pick out your knuckles. Certainly that is something you can pick out. Well, is that the sort of thing Professor Moore intended that you should pick out? It is not. And this is the test which what you pick out must satisfy in order to meet Professor Moore's requirement. You must pick out something 'with regard to which . . . it is, at first sight, a natural view to take, that that thing is identical with that part of its surface which [you are] actually seeing'. So of course, the knuckles won't do. Even the surface of the knuckles won't do. What better could one do, than pick out the surface of the hand one is seeing? Certainly you can pick this out and it would be a natural view to take that that thing is identical with that part of the surface which you are actually seeing. This is a bit doubtful however, since you would scarcely be expected to pick out the whole of the surface which you are seeing, for picking out is selecting, and after selection there would be a remainder, which in this case there would not be. Furthermore if you do pick out the surface of the hand which you are seeing, could you then (on a little reflection) doubt that it is the surface of the hand you are seeing? For until you manage to do this too you would not have picked out what Professor Moore means by a sense-datum.

I confess that I am unable with these directions to attain the desired result. Looking at my hand I can pick out knuckles, finger-

[1] Ibid., 218.

tips, nails, lines, veins, etc., but to none of them does the description which Professor Moore gives apply. If I pick out the knuckles, I am not seized with any doubts that they are the surface of my hand; and so with the finger-tips, nails, etc. And how I should ever be in a position to anticipate that what I'do pick out would satisfy the given conditions I do not understand. I can see how if yesterday I had been asked to pick out my thumb, and then a little later doubted that what I had picked out was my thumb (for I had my fingers crossed in an unusual way) then today I might, remembering, pick out what yesterday it seemed very natural to take to be identical with my thumb and then what later I came to doubt was identical with my thumb. But Professor Moore's directions are not like this. He says that there is something which you may pick out and with respect to it, you will have the described difficulty. I have not been able to pick it out.

This, then, is one peculiarity of Professor Moore's directions. One who is unacquainted with sense-data, and so has no information with regard to what to pick out, must resort to random picking, and wish for luck. Professor Moore's directions are something like this: Pick out of this basket something of which you will see that it is, at first sight, a natural view to take that that thing is identical with a red marble, but of which you will also see that it is doubtful whether it can be identical with the red marble. Now one might look at the basket and notice what there is in it. Here is a red marble, here a red pepper, here a red rubber ball, etc. One might notice all these things, and turn away, saying that there was nothing there which seemed at first glance to be a red marble, and then a moment later seemed not to be a red marble so there was nothing to pick out. On the other hand, there might be something red and round in that basket which did at first appear to be a red marble, and then upon closer inspection turned out to be a red rubber ball. And picking out the red rubber ball would satisfy the directions. I am trying by these analogies to figure out just what sort of directions these are that Professor Moore is giving, in order to show why I have been unable in looking at my hand to discover anything which I should have some reason to suppose met with Professor Moore's directions.

But this is a general comment. Professor Moore says that there is something about which you first feel sure and then about which you doubt. In seeking for this I do not see how in feeling sure one could anticipate the doubting. But I should like further to notice some peculiarities concerning what it is one is at first to be sure of, and then is to doubt. I have in mind Professor Moore's use of the following types of sentence, in which X symbolizes the something which you are able to pick out:

1. X is identical with the surface of my right hand.
2. X can be identical with the surface of my right hand.
3. X cannot be identical with the surface of my right hand.

I want first to consider the first type of sentence in order to make clear the context in which we should commonly understand it. And for this purpose I am going to define a certain word, parodying the definition which Moore gives of the word sense-datum. This is the parody:

'And in order to point out to the reader what sort of thing I mean by ——, I need only ask him to look at the cook's right hand. If he does this he will be able to pick out something with regard to which he will see that it is at first a natural view to take that that thing is identical not indeed with the cook's whole right hand, but with that part of its surface which one is actually (?) seeing but will also (on a little inspection) be able to see that it is doubtful whether it can be identical with the part of the hand in question. Things of the sort of which this thing is, which he sees in looking at the cook's hand, and with regard to which he can understand how some kitchen visitors should have supposed it to be the part of the surface of the cook's hand at which he was looking, while others have supposed that it can't be, are what I mean by rubber gloves.'

This experiment, I think, might do very well for all kitchen visitors. But obviously its success depends upon a familiarity with the use of the expression 'human hand' by which the inspection is guided. Look closely at the hand; does it look like a hand? pinch it, smell it, etc. Does the surface stretch like taffy, is it very smooth, etc? Apparently in a case such as this there is no difficulty in distinguishing the surface of a hand from the surface of rubber gloves. Now then, when the reader in Professor Moore's experiment looks at his hand, and sees the surface of his hand, what happens? Does he think that some new kind of gloves, made to resemble the hand, have come to be worn, and that these gloves are, to smell, and touch, and sight, indistinguishable from the surface of the hand, gloves which you may not know you are wearing unless you remember that you put them on? If in a case of this sort one forgot, would one then be sensing, directly perceiving, a sense-datum? The answer is: No. For what distinguishes the doubt in terms of which Professor Moore defines the sense-datum, is that it cannot be resolved. Once the doubt arises, there is no way of settling the question whether the thing one can pick out is identical with the surface of one's hand or not. It must be remembered that Professor Moore does not say that the sense-datum is not identical with the surface of the hand. He only says that in looking at one's hand one comes to doubt that something, which may be the surface of one's hand, is the surface of one's hand. But, unlike the doubt about the surface of the hand and the rubber gloves, it cannot be settled. Once the doubt has arisen, there's nothing to do but to go on doubting. Scratching, smelling, looking more closely, do not give relief.

I can imagine someone in a facetious vein suggesting that the situation which Professor Moore describes is more like trying to distinguish identical twins occupying the same space. It's as though someone had been told: 'He's identical twins', and then whenever that someone saw him, he would shake his head, looking, wondering, asking himself: Am I seeing Hans or Fritz? or when I am directly perceiving Hans, am I indirectly perceiving Fritz? He cannot decide. If someone says: You're seeing Hans, (that seems the natural view to take) he proceeds to doubt: 'Maybe it's Fritz'. He might in this situation easily come to see that some people would hold that Hans was not twins, and that Fritz is either an alternative notation for Fritz, or a meaningless expression.

Now I want to try a further experiment, again to exhibit the misleading familiarity of Professor Moore's language. In the experiment designed to test for rubber gloves, the point made was that Moore's language is applicable to such things as hands and gloves. I want now to show that it is also applicable to mirror-images. This is the experiment: 'And in order to point out to the reader what I mean by ——, I need only ask him to look into the mirror, holding up his right hand to the glass. If he does this, he will be able to pick out something with regard to which he will see, that it is, at first sight, a natural view to take, that that thing is identical, not indeed with his whole right hand, but with that part of the surface which is reflected there, but will also (smiling to himself) be able to see that it is doubtful whether it can be identical with the part of the surface of his hand in question. Things of this sort of which this thing is, which he sees in looking at the reflection of his hand, and with regard to which he can understand how some creatures, little people and puppies, should have supposed it to be the part of the surface of his hand, while grownups supposed that it can't be, are what I mean by hand-mirror-images'.

Now the point of these two analogous experiments is this: If you are among those philosophers who doubt that there are any such things as some philosophers have meant by sense-data, and if you try to understand Professor Moore's directions in the attempt to identify a sense-datum, then further if you interpret a philosopher's language as so much English, you are certain to fail. If you look at your hand and try to stir up doubts about what you are seeing, you may object to yourself: But maybe I am wearing rubber gloves. Well, you know how to take care of that. Or you may object: But maybe I am looking into a mirror, and what I see is just an image. You also know how to take care of that. What other misgiving suggestion remains then? It must be remembered that Professor Moore says that the doubt arises 'on a little reflection' though he does not, in this context at least, tell us at all what reflection induces the doubt. It won't do, of course, to object: But maybe there are sense-data, and it is a property of sense-data to pass for the surfaces of things we look at, both when and if they are, and when and if they are not, the surfaces of objects. For it is by means of some reflection which does not involve that there are sense-data, but that leads to the requisite doubt concerning the surface of one's hand, that one is persuaded that there are sense-data. What I mean to point out here is that the language of the experiment is strange language so long as we are not acquainted with sense-data. Once we distinguish a sense-datum we may come to see how it applies. But before we can do this we must come to doubt. And before we come to doubt we must indulge in a 'little reflection'. The question is: what reflection? What is it that led Professor Moore and some other philosophers to come to that pass where, when each looks at his hand, he may ask without the slightest perturbation: And is this the surface of a hand? If, actually seeing the surface of his hand, he says: 'Maybe not', then he is aware of a sense-datum. The question is: What thoughts lead him to this doubt?

Before I go on to consider what these reflections may be, I should like to discuss the second and third kinds of sentences above:

2. X can be identical with the surface of my right hand.
3. X cannot be identical with the surface of my right hand.

For this, notice a case of doubt in which one might have employed language of the sort which Professor Moore uses. Isaac on the day when he was deceived might have asked: Is this the hand of Jacob or the hand of Esau? Isaac was touching the hand and hearing the voice. The voice led him to doubt. We all understand this. And he might, had he attended Cambridge, have said: The hand that I am touching (and which I have picked out) is identical with the hand that is Esau's. I suppose that generally no one ever bothers to say a thing like this unless some doubt has preceded the assertion. So Isaac expected that this was the hand of Esau, but the voice made him doubtful. How could this be Esau's hand, when the voice which accompanied it sounded like Jacob's voice? In a dispute then, and to settle the matter (Isaac was very old!) Isaac may have said: This hand is identical with Esau's hand. He was wrong of course, but the confusion was one of hands; he mistook Jacob's hand for Esau's hand. The occasion for the use of the sentence arises after doubt and after denial. 'What do you see?' 'My right hand.' 'Oh, no you don't.' 'I say [temper rising] that what I see, is identical with my right hand. It is my right hand.' It follows, of course, that we also have a use for: X is not identical with my right hand. If Rebecca on that occasion long ago, had had a mind to, she might have interrupted with: 'You're wrong, Isaac. That hand is not identical with the hand of Esau. It's Jacob's hand.'

Now we can also make a case for 'This hand can be the hand of Esau', and so with 'This hand cannot be the hand of Esau'. Rebecca might have said: 'It can't be.' And then she would have given reasons, for such statements as 'It can be' and 'It can't be' have this sort of reference. So Isaac might have asked: Why can't it be? And the answer might have been: See here: You know that Esau's is a hairy hand. If you pull at the hairs on his hand, it pains him and you can see it on his face. And what is more the hair does not pull out. Try that experiment on this hand. There is no pain. The hair easily pulls off, and under the layer of hair, you will find paste. That's why this cannot be Esau's hand. Esau's hand is a genuine hairy, but this hand is a wolf's hand in sheep's clothing. To which Isaac might have lamented: But I thought it was Esau's. And it could have been for all I knew. The hand was hairy, it smelled of the field and of game, like Esau's hand. And it seemed like a large hand to me. So you see it could have been Esau's hand.

It is clearly, I think, situations such as these which we have in mind in the use of the expressions which Professor Moore employs. There is mistaking one thing for another thing, Jacob's hand for Esau's hand. There are also considerations which are involved in making the mistake, and other considerations which are involved in correcting the mistake. These considerations are of two kinds. If we are clear about what Jacob's hand is like, and clear about what Esau's hand is like, then the respects in which they are similar are likely to involve us in mistaking one for the other. The respects in which they are dissimilar, are the considerations which we draw upon when we correct our mistake, or when we come to say that 'This cannot be so and so'.

Accordingly, when Professor Moore says that you can pick out something about which you are inclined to say that it is identical with the surface of your hand, and this arises in a context in which you are inclined to say both that it can be, and that it cannot be, one would expect that some reasons would be at hand in respect to both. What makes you think that what you can pick out, can be identical with the surface of your hand and what makes you think that it cannot be identical with it? Is what you picked out similar in certain respects to the surface of your right hand, and dissimilar in certain other respects to that surface? Professor Moore has said that one would come to doubt by way of 'a little reflection', as I noticed before, and the analysis which we have just made would lead one to expect that the reflection would consist in noticing similarities and dissimilarities between what you picked out and the surface of your right hand. Of course, if any dissimilarities were noticed, that ought to settle the matter. If the something is dissimilar, then of course, it is not the surface of one's hand. It looks as though one is aware of nothing but similarities, supposing one has picked out something, and yet that one is suspicious that there may be dissimilarities of which one is unaware. It's as though one were looking at one's hand, and had a suspicion that what one was seeing was not one's hand at all. So one examined one's hand carefully, found out that it was exactly what one expected one's hand to be like and yet concluded: 'But maybe there is something I am not seeing, maybe there's a difference I am missing. So maybe after all, this is not my hand.' What then planted this suspicion?

There is one further point that I should like to make. The experiment which Professor Moore proposes, takes for granted that each of us knows how to identify the surface of his hand. It is in terms of this identification that we are to come to recognize the something we pick out. Now then, each of us is able to describe his own hand. One might take a print of it, study it carefully for colour shadings, shape and surface markings. If then one is well-informed about the surface of one's own hand, the doubt which Professor Moore describes does not arise because of any lack of information about one's hand. Apparently then the something which you pick out has the same characteristics which the surface of your hand has. If it did not have the same characteristics, obviously it would be different from the surface of your hand, and if it had the same and some others, it would also be different. So, if it has any characteristics at all, it must have the same characteristics as the surface of your hand. How then explain the suggestion that they are different? Are they in different places? This is also out of the question. We do not see the surface of the hand in one place, and pick out the something in a different place. If we did, the doubt that the 'something' and the surface of my hand are identical would be settled. This too does not explain the suggestion that the something and the surface of my hand are identical. What then?

If what I have just suggested about knowing the surface of one's hand is not admitted, then what? Then certainly we are at a loss. The experiment presupposes that we know something, and that by way of this we may become aware of something else. If you know the surface of your hand, you can become acquainted with your knuckles. You certainly can, if you look at your hand, pick out your knuckles. In some such way as this you also become acquainted with 'a sense-datum'. Suppose however that, in a situation in which you did pick out your knuckles, you were seized with a doubt as to whether your knuckles were identical with the surface of your right hand which you are seeing, how would you account for this? If nothing very serious has happened, one might suggest that you had now come to use the expression 'the surface of my hand' in a very unusual way. I have an inkling that something of this sort has happened in the sentences from Professor Moore's exposition. If one can think that 'the something which one can pick out' is identical with the surface of one's hand, then either one must take for granted the use of the expression 'the surface of one's hand' which applies then to something one can see, smell, touch, kiss, etc., and so grant that what one can pick out is also something which one can see, smell, touch, kiss, etc., or otherwise one takes for granted the use of the expression 'what one can pick out' knowing well what this is like that one can pick out, and that for instance one cannot touch, taste, smell, etc., what one can pick out, and so grant also that 'the surface of my hand' is something which, like what one can pick out, can be seen, but cannot be touched, tasted, smelled, etc. Either, then, Professor Moore is in effect saying that you can pick out a physical object which is identical with the surface of your hand, or you can pick out something which is not a physical object at all, and that is identical with the surface of your hand. The puzzle is as to how a non-physical object (a sense-datum) can be identical with a physical object. It seems at any rate inevitable that if anything can be conceived to be the surface of my hand, it must be physical; and that if the surface of my hand can be conceived to be a sense-datum, the surface of my hand is not physical. But in that case what has happened to the expression: 'the surface of my hand'?

II

I have tried, in what preceded, to point out some of the difficulties which I have met in trying to follow Professor Moore's directions. And I regard as crucial in this respect the three sentences which I discussed, and the use of the phrase: 'the surface of my hand'. I also noticed that what leads to the doubt in Professor Moore's experiment, is a 'little reflection'. My suggestion is that it is the same 'little reflection' which leads us to use these sentences, and the phrase just noticed. And I want now to describe the reflections which, in my own case, seem to lead me in that direction.

There are especially three sets of facts which lead me to try to distinguish a sense-datum in the prescribed way. One is certain facts concerning sounds, odours and tastes. Another is facts concerning mirror reflections, images, echoes, etc. And a third is the use of such expressions as: It looks like . . . , This looks like . . . , etc. There may be other facts which are relevant as these are. But I have noticed that when I, at any rate, meet the expression sense-data, these are the sorts of fact which come to my mind.

I want, before I go on, to notice how narrowly Professor Moore has conceived the problem of sense-data. It is common among those who say that there are sense-data to say that sounds, odours, tastes, etc., are sense-data; but it appears, apart from the tell-no-tale phrase 'in a certain respect', that Professor Moore means by a sense-datum only that sort of thing which may be taken to be the surface of something or other. In other words, Professor Moore confines his use of the phrase sense-datum only to what others would describe as *visual* sense-data. I find Professor Moore's definition unusual in this respect, or misleading. If he does define 'sense-data' in such a way as to include only 'visual sense-data' then he defines the term in a way inconsistent with his own use of the term, for in a previous sentence he says, referring to sense-data: 'I am at present seeing a great number of them and feeling others.' At any rate his exposition excludes smells, tastes, and sounds. However that may be, the problem here is: What reflections would lead one to distinguish something which one would then say can or cannot be identical with the surface of one's hand which one is seeing?

The fact with respect to sounds, smells, and tastes is that they function in perceptual experiences in two ways. I can illustrate this best by a few pairs of sentences. Notice these:

I hear a gnawing sound.
I hear a rat.

I smell an odour.
I smell a rat.

I taste a sour taste.
I taste a lemon.

The first of each of these pairs functions independently of the second, and one can describe sounds, odours, and tastes, without committing oneself to any sentence of the sort which is second in each pair. But the second does not function independently of the first. If you say: I hear a rat, then the question: What was the sound like?, is pertinent. In each case one may ask: What was the sound, or the odour, or the taste like? We are all acquainted with the descriptions of sounds, odours, and tastes. I need not, I think, enlarge upon this. If now someone held that there were sense-data and he meant by this that there were sounds, odours, and tastes, and that these are descriptively independent of rats and lemons, etc., there would, I think, be no controversy about this. There is no such question as: Is the sound or the odour of the rat identical with the surface of a rat, or the taste of a lemon identical with the surface of a lemon, or of that part of the lemon which I am tasting?

But now there are also certain similarities among facts of this following sort:
I hear a rat.
I smell a rat.
I taste a lemon.
I see a cloud.
I touch velvet.

And here, I take it, one is likely by reflection upon these sets of similarities to suppose that there must be some fact which corresponds to: I see a cloud, as: I hear a sound corresponds to: I hear a rat. And so too with: I touch velvet. Since, in other words, to hearing there corresponds a hearing sense-datum, and to smelling a smelling sense-datum, etc., so to seeing and to touching there must correspond seeing and touching sense-data. Actually, of course, there need not be such; and one part of the suggested parallel between hearing, smelling, and tasting, on the one hand, and seeing and touching, on the other, is missing. There are no descriptions of 'sights' and 'touches' which are independent conceptually of the descriptive characteristics of rats, lemons, clouds, velvet, etc. If you attempt to describe what you see, the same words which you use to describe the lemon or the cloud, will also serve to describe the purported sense-datum. So, if there is a sense-datum in these last cases, a new vocabulary will have to be engaged to perform the service. And so we get two different meanings for 'is red' in the sentences 'This (sense-datum) is red', and 'This rose is red'. This sort of accommodation is the consequence of the assumption that just as there are auditory sense-data so there must be visual sense-data. We make up for the deficiency in the facts from which we start by inventing a new vocabulary. Unfortunately we are compelled to use the same words which have otherwise performed an unambiguous service. It also follows that, if in the respect noted, seeing is like hearing, then as one is able, in hearing a bird, to distinguish the sound of the bird, so in seeing a hand one is able to pick out a corresponding visual sense-datum. The effect of these analogies may be so strong as to lead one to say that there must be a sense-datum.

These analogies do not however provide the only motive. Consider mirror reflections. Mirror reflections are like sounds and odours and tastes in a certain respect, and they are like lemons and clouds and velvet in another respect. The image of a lemon or a cloud is like a sound or an odour, in that the image is descriptively independent of the description of any lemon or cloud. On the other hand, the description of an image of a lemon or cloud is unlike the description of a sound or odour, in that the descriptive items which compose it are engaged also in describing lemons and clouds. Now how do these facts about images incline one to the belief that when one is looking at one's hand one is seeing a sense-datum, as one hears a sound? Perhaps in this way: If one is already impressed with the analogy between hearing and seeing, then one is inclined to believe that there is something which one is seeing which is distinguishable as the sound is from the bird one hears. Now if you look at your hand and try to discover this corresponding element, you may find your effort encouraged by the fact that there are things which are descriptively identical with what you are seeing which are nevertheless not the surfaces of lemons and clouds at all. That is, here you have in reflections what, since they are described in the same way in which lemons and clouds and hands are described, may very well be taken to be 'the surfaces of lemons and clouds'. So when you look at your hand, you may describe what you see just as you would describe the reflection of it in the mirror. Since then what you see is taken to be the surface of your hand, you at once understand how something might be described in this same way, and yet not be the surface of your hand at all. For the image in the mirror is not the surface of your hand. It is clear certainly that with this in mind you can, if you look at your hand, pick out something which is like what you saw in the mirror, when you raised your hand to the mirror.

There is one further set of facts which disposes us in the same way. Notice such sentences as these:

This sounds like a horse.

This smells like an onion.

This tastes like a peppermint.

This looks like a million dollars.

This feels like a sponge.

The use of these expressions is parallel to the first set described above. The first three are admittedly statements about a sound, a smell, and a taste. Now how about the fourth and the fifth? Well, they must also be about a 'look' and about a 'feel', the corresponding sense-data of seeing and touching, respectively. This does not now seem to me at all persuasive, and of course, for the same reason which I gave in discussing sounds, smells, etc. If one wished, for instance, to identify by description or by some other form of direction, the sound or smell in question, as distinguished from the horse or the onion, this is a simple matter. But if you wish to call attention to the 'look' or to the 'feel' in question there is no resort to doing this, save pointing out or identifying the 'million dollars' or 'the sponge' or whatever the object may be. In other words, what is called the 'look' or the 'feel' is not identifiable in the way in which the sound, or smell are identifiable. The use of the word 'this' is commonly defined so as to apply to such uses as are involved in these first three sentences. But it is only by analogy that one comes to suppose that in the last two sentences the use is like that in the first three. Of course such a sentence as: 'This looks like a million dollars', may apply also to a mirror-image, and we have already noticed what this means. The image of a girl who looks like a million dollars would also look like a million dollars. This means simply that they are described in the same way. Certainly from such facts as these, which we all admit, it does not follow that when you look at your hand, you can pick out something which is not your hand, of which you now say that it looks like your hand.

These are some of the facts upon which I reflect a little, when I am led to the view that what Professor Moore has tried to persuade us is true. I want now to show that, if one does follow the lead of these facts, one is likely to use precisely the sort of language about 'sense-data' which Professor Moore does use. If the analogy between seeing and hearing holds, then it follows in the first place that if you look at your right hand you will be able to pick out something, something which on the assumption given, corresponds to the sound in hearing. But this is a strange sort of direction, for, if I look at my right hand, nothing at all corresponds to the sound in case of hearing. There is simply my hand, or more conveniently as you will see in a moment, the surface of my hand. So I pick that out. Now I reflect, and describe what I see, reminded that what I see is like reflections in mirrors. I know, of course, that mirror-reflections are not identical with the surfaces of any hands, no matter how perfect the image may be. Now, since this is like an image in all these respects, it can't be the surface of my hand at all, and this in spite of the fact that I thought at the outset that I was picking out the surface of my hand. If the only thing I could pick out was what I took to be the surface of my hand, and that is the sense-datum, and this is like the image in the mirror, then see what follows. The reflection in the mirror has no depth. I cannot prick it with a pin. Now then does the surface of my hand have depth? If you say that what you picked out is like the reflection in the mirror, and it has no depth, then if it is identical with the surface of my hand, then the surface of my hand also has no depth. Can that be? On the other hand, if you say that what I picked out is identical with the surface of my hand, and the surface of my hand has depth, are we then to allow that the sense-datum, like a hand's surface, has depth? Can I prick a sense-datum with a pin? This is the puzzle which I noticed previously when I discussed Professor Moore's use of the phrase 'surface of my hand', and it arises from conceiving of the sense-datum as like a mirror-reflection, and at the same time as something which one can pick out. If then, on this basis, I look at my hand, and try to pick out a sense-datum, I must be surprised to discover something which, though it may be in certain respects like the image in the mirror, is also remarkably unlike it. For, in spite of what all these facts already noticed lead me to expect, I discover nothing but my hand.

I should like to labour this last point. Imagine the sort of situation you would be in, if, upon the basis of such facts as I have noticed, you were disposed to expect a sense-datum. What would you say in trying to describe what you expect? First of all, you might tell someone to look at his hand, on the expectation that just as if he heard a bird, there would be a sound to identify, so here there would be something corresponding to the sound. It also follows from the character of what you see, that if there is something corresponding to the sound, then you could pick it out. If this were all, one would be inclined to describe what you might pick out as 'a yellow patch', 'a red patch', 'a canoid patch of brown', etc., and it is easy to see what in a case of this sort has happened. People who invent expressions of this sort are trying to find some expressions which parallel the descriptions of sounds, but the parallel is deceptive. For, if in looking at your hand you now try to pick out 'a hand-shape of pink', you will find yourself picking out the surface of your hand, whereas in the case of a sound the relations between the sound and the bird are obviously different. The description of the sound is not a description of the bird. But there is no necessity for pursuing this. It is only necessary that what you pick out should, like the sound, be distinguishable from your hand, or the surface of your hand. As it is, you know that reflections in mirrors and images otherwise are distinguishable from what they reflect and image, though they are not descriptively distinguishable from what they reflect and image. So we formulate a description accordingly: Pick out what has the characteristics of a mirror-reflection. Looking into the mirror, holding your hand to the mirror, I might ask: What do you see?, and what you would then give me as a description would equally apply to your hand. Now then you look at your hand, and describe your hand, for what will satisfy my request is just that. Further, if you have already committed yourself to saying that there is something here which corresponds to the sound in the case of hearing the bird, then you will feel pretty sure that you have picked that out. But you will nevertheless be puzzled. For if you have picked out the sense-datum, then if someone says: Now pick out the surface of your hand, you will be unable to do so unless the sense-datum and the surface of your hand are identical. And if you then ask: Did I pick out the surface of my hand?, already assured that you did pick out the sense-datum, you will be inclined to say: That may be, for a sense-datum can be the surface of a hand. And you will be inclined to say this because, as I said before, the reflection and the surface of my hand are similar. But you will also be inclined to say that a sense-datum cannot be the surface.

III

I have tried, in the preceding sections, first of all to explore certain difficulties in the directions which Professor Moore gives for discovering what it is he means by a sense-datum, and second to try to discover what motives there are which lead us to expect that there are sense-data, and which lead us also to such curious descriptions of them. My thesis has been this: The obvious distinction between sounds, tastes, and smells in hearing, tasting, and smelling leads us to expect a corresponding something or other in the case of seeing and touching. So when I look at my hand, I am led to expect that there is a sense-datum in this case. So I may say that I can pick it out. But when I try to pick it out I am at a loss. There is only my hand. Now if I still persist in holding that there is a sense-datum present, I am bound to describe it in a peculiar way. I am likely to describe it in analogy with an image or mirror-reflection. I may go on to think of the sense-datum which must be there, as spread exceedingly thin over the surface of my hand, a kind of epi-epidermis, and at the same time as looking just like my hand when the sense-datum has been removed. Now if I keep this fixed in my mind, and look at my hand, and if I am asked: What do you see?, I am supposed not to know what to say. Do I see just an image spread over the surface of my hand like so much surfacing surfaceless paint, or do I see the surface of my hand? I think I can tell an image from the surface of my hand, but I confess that I should be much distressed in the attempt to distinguish the image of the surface of my hand laid neatly on the surface of my hand and defined in such a way as to be indistinguishable from the surface of my hand, from the surface of my hand. But fortunately, as I think, at least, I am not led to expect anything like images spread over the surface of my hand, and if I did, I should try pricking the epidermis. As I have noticed before, that the attempt to describe what 'must' be present is desperate is also apparent in the consequent use of the expression 'the surface of his hand'. For we do not as a matter of fact have any difficulty in identifying the surface of our hands. If then there is some difficulty, that difficulty has not been properly described. And the point of my essay is that the supposed entity which is defined in terms of a confusion, which is generated by sentential likenesses, misleads us and catches us in linguistic pockets.

Rubber gloves, the image of my hand, another man's hand, all of these I know how to distinguish from my hand, when I look at my hand, and when I am in doubt. But I am not moved by the suggestion that whenever I look at my hand an image of my hand may be interposed between my hand and my eye. In that case we should need to invent the theory of the Pre-Established Harmony between the hand and the sense-datum. But why suggest it?

Having come to the end of my essay I am now full of misgivings. I know that I have not refuted Professor Moore's view. I have tried however, teasing the words of Professor Moore's exposition, to get the matter straight. And this is what has come of it. May my betters rob me of my 'darling follies', among which betters I have long counted first Professor Moore.

II
THE DIFFERENCE BETWEEN SENSING
AND OBSERVING

1. R. J. Hirst[1]

THE EXISTENCE of sense-data, or even of sensations other than pains, itches and the like, has been so strongly challenged of late that we shall have to consider carefully whether the main difference between sensing and observing is not simply that the former is a myth. As the claim that sensing occurs is advanced by the sense-datum theories above all—indeed the word is largely their technical term—I shall devote much of this paper to an examination of their main variants. I shall in fact reject them and the case they make out for sensing, but merely to do this would be philosophically unsatisfying, for they are but one attempt to formulate the traditional distinction between the sensory and the interpretative elements in perception—a fundamental problem which seems to me to underlie and give significance to the subject of this symposium. In the last section, therefore, I shall consider the main psychological and physiological arguments for the thesis that observing involves having sensations, and try to show that, though their usual conclusion is not justified, they do afford grounds for distinguishing within observing a more basic mode of awareness which might well be called sensing.[2]

Before attempting this I must say a little about the word 'observe'. In its ordinary usage it is very ambiguous, and although

Symposium by R. J. Hirst and Richard Wollheim. From *Proceedings of the Aristotelian Society*, Supp. Vol. 28 (1954), pp. 97–240. Reprinted by courtesy of the authors and the Editor of the Aristotelian Society.

[1] [This paper gave an early version of views which the writer later developed more fully. A more extended treatment is to be found in his books, *The Problems of Perception* and (with Wyburn and Pickford) *Human Senses and Perception*, Part III (see Bibliography). Ed.]

[2] Several topics here discussed have been dealt with in my article in *Mind* (1951), but with some differences, mainly of emphasis and terminology. A few of my present arguments are stated more fully there.

Professor Ryle finds it convenient in that it can cover both task and achievement in perception, whereas 'perceive', like 'see' and 'hear', only covers achievements,[1] this convenience seems to me to be outweighed by the danger of *Ignoratio Elenchi*; if philosophers to be criticized for confusing sensation and observation have been concerned only with the analysis of veridical and illusory perceiving, i.e., of achievement in observation, it seems beside the point continually to emphasize how observing in its task sense (watching or listening) differs from sensation.[2] Besides this and other ambiguities the ordinary usage of 'observe' is too narrow in that it seems largely confined to seeing—one cannot observe a symphony with one's ears or sherry with one's tongue—and too wide in that one can observe by means of meters what is wholly beyond the reach of one's senses. Hence to do justice to the philosophical problem before us we must use the word in a specialized meaning, though without following those philosophers who have used it as an equivalent to 'sense' or 'immediately perceive'[3]—an arbitrary usage which would leave us nothing to discuss. Hence I propose, provisionally at least, to use 'observe' interchangeably with 'perceive' as a generic term for the seeing, hearing and so on of physical objects. Once we have discovered the difference, if any, between sensing and this kind of observing, we can add a rider to the effect that the word can also be used in a task sense.

There is a further difficulty that 'perceive' and 'observe' normally imply both a mode of consciousness and the existence of its appropriate object. 'He saw a book on the table' implies both an awareness on his part and the existence of the book on the table, whereas 'He thought he saw a book' implies error, e.g., that it was really a disguised flask. I shall follow Price's terminology for the awareness, and say 'He was perceptually conscious of a book', when I do not wish to imply either veridical perception or error; but all who do so must beware of the dangerous ambiguity in 'conscious of'. This can be used as a mere synonym of 'perceive', i.e., so as to imply the existence of that of which one is conscious, a usage which must be rigorously excluded from 'perceptually conscious of'. When I use 'perceive' and 'observe' I shall imply both awareness and existence of the physical object.

---

[1] *The Concept of Mind*, p. 233.
[2] Cf. op. cit. pp. 203–4 or 237–8.
[3] E.g., Moore, *Philosophical Studies*, p. 68; or Ayer, *Language, Truth and Logic*, 2nd ed., pp. 11–12, where 'observation-statements' record sense-contents.

I

On the classical theory of sense-data, which I will consider in the form it takes in Price's *Perception*, sensing and observing may be distinguished briefly as follows: sensing is direct awareness of sense-data, i.e., of colour patches, sounds, smells, etc., while perceptual consciousness involves this and a further mental act or process, the taking for granted or rational belief that there is present to the senses the material object specified by the sense-data; when the material object is so present this consciousness amounts to observing, to a mediated awareness of the object.

Sensing is the fundamental activity and is often described as a form of knowing, for its essential features are immediacy and certainty. When I see a tomato, for example, I may doubt whether it is a tomato or an imitation or an hallucination, but I cannot doubt 'that there exists a red patch of a round and somewhat bulgy shape . . . ',[1] viz., a sense-datum. This belief, that there is always in perceiving an immediate, incorrigible and so unvaryingly excellent awareness of an existent, I have called the 'immediacy assumption'; it might be fairer to call it a claim, since it is asserted that if we make an analysis of the type Price makes we cannot but recognize this awareness.

But his is not the only analysis possible, nor I think the most plausible one. First there is the general difficulty that from the mere introspective analysis of any such experience nothing seems to follow about the *existence* of any object. Though the term 'existence' is not further specified in the tomato example, the use of terms like 'knowledge by acquaintance' or 'belonging to a material object' requires a degree of distinct and potentially independent existence[2] which would need the correlation of a number of experiences to establish it. Thus although there seems to be awareness of a red existent we cannot be absolutely certain of this, for the experience may in fact be 'adverbial' as is indeed claimed by some of sensing. Secondly, in the actual example our doubts about the object of awareness are due to a knowledge of the possibilities, which may be reduced to two, that we are perceiving or are having hallucinations; and the alleged certainty must depend on there being the same type of object in the two situations. But if we are perceiving, then the object of our

---

[1] *Perception*, p. 3.
[2] Ibid. pp. 43–44, concerning independent existence. (I do not think the author would now be so brusque about adverbial analyses.)

awareness is a public physical object, e.g., a tomato on the table, a tomato seen in, i.e., via, a mirror, a piece of wax or cardboard of the shape and colour of a tomato, or part of a painted canvas or illuminated screen. If we are having an hallucination, then on the most plausible theory we are having a mental image which we fail to distinguish from perceived objects; the mental image, being private, is probably the content of an 'adverbial' experience, but even if it is not we have no right to assume that it is a red existent of the same type as what we are aware of in the perceptual situation. Thirdly, although in describing perceptions we may loosely say we see 'something red over there', we cannot strictly say this, but only 'something red or at least red-looking', for the object may be some other colour and only be looking red in this light. It may be replied that the analysis is concerned with sensible colour not physical colour. But you cannot say that sensible means sensed, in Price's meaning of the word, without begging the question; to describe sensible qualities is rather to speak phenomenologically, to describe how a thing looks without implying that it has or has not the quality in question. So to say that the sensible colour is an existent, that there exists a red particular different from the physical object characterized, is to go beyond what is revealed in the experience, and seems rather to be a hypostatization of the look of the object.

We may underline this point by mentioning Price's attempt to defend 'primary recognition' from the charge that it is sensing in a new guise.[1] In his example of the bird my objection would be to the admission, if we are speaking strictly, that any existent was characterized by black; there was a black-looking object all right, namely the bird, but its actual colour may have been dark green or blue; if we are not to presuppose the sense-datum theory we must say that primary recognition is of how the object looks and not necessarily of its actual qualities, although of course the person recognizing will probably not distinguish between 'is' and 'looks' black.

To return to the tomato: it is still a far cry from the claim that something red exists to the assertion that it is a sense-datum, in view of the characteristics which sense-data are alleged to possess, viz., privacy, transitoriness and lack of causal properties. That the 'something' has these characteristics is admittedly not to be discovered in the experience itself, but is part of the theory developed to explain illusions and hallucinations. These can however be explained without invoking sense-data.

[1] *Thinking and Experience*, pp. 49–50.

Hallucinations, as I have mentioned, may be regarded as mental images confused with or taken for perceived objects; the occurrence of this mistake is explained by there being always some factor which lessens the difference normally obvious between the two, or makes us incapable of recognizing it, e.g., fever, madness, *delirium tremens*, drowsiness, prior suggestion, unusually vivid imagery or bad light. Thus, to take a favourite case, the drunkard has not normal powers of discrimination and so cannot distinguish having vivid pink images from seeing real rats; 'incorrigible' is the last word to apply to his cognitive faculties, however appropriate it is to his morals, and so we cannot admit that he senses pink rat-like existents, instead of merely imagining them. Having hallucinations is not then observing or sensing sense-data; it does not enter into the analysis of observing and should be classed rather with dreaming or having imagery—though a complete theory of perception must account for the subjective similarity of such states of mind to perceiving. We must also distinguish having after images from observing; their privacy is unchallenged and they cannot be avoided by looking elsewhere or closing the eyes; they are not thus typical sense-data—or if they are we do not sense sense-data in perceiving—and are the after effects of certain perceptions, not cases of perceiving.

Nor is a sense-datum theory required for illusions if one does not make the immediacy claim. In the penny situation there is no elliptical existent at all, and so no private transitory one, unless that claim is accepted—there is simply a round penny looking elliptical, in one sense of 'look', just because it is seen from an oblique angle. The colour-blind man has defective eyesight and so a red object looks grey to him; but there is no grey existent and so no private grey one, unless we assume that despite defective sense organs he still incorrigibly senses. Similarly in double vision the convergence of the eyes is spoilt by drink or by pressing on the eyeball, so that an object looks double;[1] even if we insist on saying that there appear to the victim to be two objects instead of one, this does not mean that there are two or that he sees two existents with the same reliability as that with which normal persons see one. In all such cases the object looks different from what it really is, because the percipient gets a distorted, distant or indirect view of it owing to his position or intervening media, and so has no optimum incorrigible awareness of it, or because he cannot see or hear it properly owing to defects of the sense

[1] I cannot see why '"double" is not really a predicate at all'; there are double chins, pyrethrums, stars, axes and eagles.

organs.[1] The sense-datum theory, however, has to explain distortions and indistinct or unclear seeing and hearing as due to changes in the object of a constantly incorrigible awareness. Not only does this involve postulating a host of unnecessary existents instead of the simpler hypothesis of an awareness of varying quality, but it is particularly unplausible when there are defects in the sense organs which must surely reduce the excellence of sensory awareness. We must also remember that the favourite examples of sense-data, coloured shapes and sounds, may be seen or heard indistinctly as well as distinctly, so that such failures cannot be blamed on the activities alleged to convert sensing to observing.

A similar point arises with respect to attention: Price himself rightly claims that when we attend to an object and as a result see it as a determinate shade of green instead of green or coloured in general, the change is not in the colour itself but in our mode of apprehension of it;[2] but if the sense-datum was peacock-green all the time, how can our original inattentive awareness of it be described as 'knowing', or as 'sensing' even, if 'sensing exists in full perfection or not at all'?[3] Such high claims for sensing, seem quite inconsistent with the admission sometimes made with respect to 'the problem of the speckled hen' that sense-data may have properties that they do not appear to have. But the situation is worse even than that—consider a pink expanse belonging to a wallpaper or to a picture in a cheaply printed book; it clearly appears to have the property pink, to be a pink sense-datum, but if we look closely we see that it is really red dots on a white background; has then this variegated sense-datum appeared to have a property, uniform pink, that it has not got? The theory seems to face a fatal dilemma—either change in attention is unplausibly explained as a change in the object and not in the mode of apprehension, or else sensing is not incorrigible, is not knowing, and its *raison d'être* has disappeared.

This difficulty is largely avoided by another well-known account,

---

[1] Note the weakness of Ryle's argument that 'see', 'perceive', etc., are achievement words because a person cannot see incorrectly and 'the perception verb itself connotes that he did not go wrong'. (*Concept of Mind*, p. 238, cp. p. 222.) It seems merely a linguistic accident that we designate perceptual shortcomings by 'indistinctly', 'not clearly', 'not properly' and not by 'incorrectly'. The task/achievement distinction does however point to a genuine and long recognized distinction between seeing and looking or watching, and to the fact that 'I see X' implies X exists.

[2] *Perception*, pp. 16–17.

[3] Ibid. p. 149.

which can explain such changes as changes in our mode of sensing. It denies that there is an act/object distinction in sensing, and claims that 'I sense a red expanse' is a statement about how I sense, which might be expressed by paraphrasing adverbially, 'I sense redly', or by saying that 'red expanse' is an internal accusative, since the red cannot exist apart from the sensing any more than a blow can from the striking of it. But this view, like the classical sense-datum theory, is put forward as the fundamental fact of a perceptual situation; whatever in view of illusions and so on we may doubt, we cannot doubt that sense-experiences of this kind occur, and so we must analyse our concept of material object in terms of them. But the fact that there are two rival analyses of sensing shows that they cannot both be indubitable and correct—perhaps neither is. The difficulty with this adverbial analysis is that I do not see how anyone can simply by analysing his experiences deny the prima facie obvious act/object distinction within a perceptual situation. Seeing and touching do not seem adverbial but seem to be awareness of an external object; so a mere denial of this carries little weight and would have to be supported by arguments to show that we are deceived in this, and the most likely ones are inferences from physiology illegitimate on this theory.

Both accounts of sensing, however, seem open to a further objection. Sense-data are alleged to be private objects or experiences and to have no causal properties, yet the standard examples of them are colour expanses, sounds and smells. But all these seem as public as tables or chairs—two or more people can smell the same smell or hear the same sound. In favourable circumstances two observers will agree as to the exact location of a coloured expanse and as to the time, duration and location of a noise, so, physiological considerations apart, there seems no reason to deny that they are quantitatively as well as qualitatively the same colour or sound. They also may have causal properties: a sound can break a wine glass or activate a microphone, and in a well-known school experiment colour alone affects the absorption of heat by a tin box. Indeed if colour patches or sounds are private and non-causal how can they be respectively photographed or recorded? In this they are a marked contrast to dreams and mental images to which these epithets may plausibly be applied.

It may be said that this is unfair since physiology shows that colours and sounds are private sensations and that what is public is their cause. I hope it will be clear later that this is a misleading interpretation of the physiological evidence, but even if it were true one could

still accuse the sense-datum theories of a ὕστερον πρότερον, in that
these physiological arguments should then have been their starting
point; they would however spurn the support of such dubious
arguments. We may note that the adverbial analysis especially seems in
difficulties about public qualities. If when two people claim to be
seeing the same colour they are simply having qualitatively similar
but quantitatively different colour experiences, then one can hardly
leave this as an unexplained coincidence, like two persons dreaming
the same dream but strangely more frequent; that would be even more
incredible when one considered that it was only when they looked in
the same direction that such coincidences occurred, or tried to
explain a photograph of that same colour. So it would seem that to
avoid postulating endless series of inexplicable coincidences one has
to say, like Locke, that there is an unobservable public cause, or to
bring in a *deus ex machina* to arrange a pre-established harmony of
people's sensations.[1] Either expedient spells bankruptcy.

II

So far I have tried to show that these accounts of sensing have failed
to establish the actual occurrence of the activity described, so that it
would be fruitless to consider further how this alleged activity is
related to observing. In all this I have treated these accounts as
theories of perception, since they seem to me to be attempts to discover the facts of perception, to explain them and solve the problems
to which they give rise. It has, however, been denied that they are
theories of this type—they are only variants of a 'sense-datum
language' which is an alternative to the everyday so-called 'material
object language', and is just a better terminology for expressing the
facts of perception on which we are all agreed. This would mean that
the main difference between 'sensing' and 'observing' is that they
belong to different languages.

The main reason adduced for demoting theories of perception to
languages is that 'each of them will cover any known fact; but none
of them enables us to make any inference at all from the known to the
unknown'.[2] But this does not make them merely languages. I do not
see why the same stringent standards of predictive fruitfulness should
be demanded of philosophical theories as of scientific ones. The
latter normally have a subject-matter admitting a mathematical

---

[1] As Berkeley was tempted to do, see *Principles*, 30ff. or 61ff.
[2] Ayer, *The Foundations of Empirical Knowledge*, p. 53.

treatment which makes precise deduction and testing easier; philosophers of perception may have to be satisfied with a different type of explanation, namely a systematization of all the facts which renders them intelligible and free from problems. Anyhow, as the offering of criteria of simplicity shows, even in science there is always the possibility that two rival hypotheses explain all the known facts but nothing can be deduced from them to enable one to choose between them; this happened for a time in the case of the Ptolemaic and Copernican hypotheses.

Furthermore, to call the sense-datum theory a language is to imply that it does not postulate new facts or introduce a new conception of known ones. But the adoption of any variant of the theory involves most of the following suppositions: that there are unsuspected existents which are private objects of awareness in perception differing from physical objects; that all perceiving, even when one cannot see or hear clearly, involves incorrigible knowledge of some existent; that colours, sounds, smells, etc., are private and wholly without causal properties; that seeing a colour is an adverbial experience in which no object can be distinguished from the act; and that hallucinations are to be classed with perceptions not mental images. These involve taking sides on matters of fact—the first four against common sense, the last against many psychologists. Hence the alleged sense-datum language is concealed theory, and indeed in explaining the terms used in it its sponsors have openly supported one of the two analyses of experience I have rejected, usually the adverbial one.

It is instructive also to consider the advantages claimed for the sense-datum language. At first it was asserted to be necessary for a proper account of illusions and hallucinations, but attention to normal usage has scotched that by showing that ordinary language can adequately describe them; (it would be strange if it could not). In the latest statement of the view[1] the main claim is that the sense-datum language is so much neater than its distractingly clumsy rivals that it is indispensable for detailed phenomenological description. But such description would normally be carried out by talking of coloured shapes, patches of light and shade, sounds of such and such pitch and tone, etc., i.e., in ordinary language with the recognized convention

---

[1] Price in *Aristotelian Society Supplementary Volume*, xxvi (1952), p. 233. He calls it 'sensation language' to include the adverbial analysis, but my 'sense-datum language' is meant to do that too.

that it is neutral in such contexts and does not imply the existence
of material objects. Why should the sense-datum theorists be allowed
to appropriate such language? If it is neutral it is also neutral in not
implying that the shapes and sounds are private existences or
'adverbial'. They could only claim special credit for such language if
its use inevitably implied their account of the nature of colours, shapes
and sounds, which would mean that it was the expression of a theory,
not merely a language. A further claim is that 'sensation language'
is needed by scientists and psychologists for discussing the causation
of perception. This would be denied by Gestalt psychologists and is
anyhow an odd recommendation in view of the opprobrium usually
heaped on such gentlemen and their causal theories by epistemologists. More important, the 'sensations' of the psychologists and
physiologists are by no means the same as sense-data, and so do not
support a sense-datum language, e.g., they are defined as experiences
caused by the action of objects on the sense organs, and tend to be
allotted the supposed qualities of the stimulus rather than of the
'look' of the object, where, as in object constancy, there seems to be
a difference;[1] in such cases their postulation is clearly a matter of
theory not language.

Since the alternative language theory is thus generally inadequate
as an account or defence of sensing, it is *a fortiori* unable to solve our
present problem. A final and more specific objection would be this:
if the sense-datum language really is a true alternative to material
object language, if they really are two ways of saying the same thing,
then presumably 'I saw a tomato on the table' says the same as 'I
sensed a red patch of round and bulgy shape in a brown sensefield',
or as a group of statements of that type. But it is clear that on any of
the normal explanations of 'sense' equivalence of single sentences is
impossible, while equivalence of one ordinary statement with a group
of sensing ones would weaken the claim to neatness. Worse still,
almost all philosophers have recognized that perceiving is more than
just having purely sensory experiences and involves some non-sensory
activity. Opinions have admittedly differed about what this is—
interpretation, synthesis, taking for granted or what—but once it is
admitted, as I hope we shall see it must be, then statements solely
about sensings, even a group of them, cannot be equivalent to a

---

[1] Views differ as would be expected in a question of theory, but for this kind
of account of sensations see Woodworth, *Psychology* (18th ed.), p. 465 or his *Experimental Psychology*, p. 450, or Boring, Langfield and Weld, *Introduction to Psychology*,
p. 496.

statement about observing, since they cannot do justice to its non-sensory element.

III

We have thus rejected the main current theories of sensing, but are faced with the question: can observing be analysed into some non-sensory activity working on a different kind of sensing? Before proceeding we must note the view that this cannot be done, that observing is unanalysable so that the problem before us is based on a misconception. This, the so-called 'percept theory', is summed up in James's dictum 'a perception is one state of mind or nothing',[1] and rests on the claim that by direct inspection of perceptual consciousness we are unable to discover any core of sensing. But although this seems plausible with regard to sight it seems to neglect the other senses; it seems to me that one can distinguish a sound or a smell quite easily from its source, and that, except in familiar and so presumably automatic cases, one can distinguish within consciousness of the source both the hearing of the sound and some judgment as to its source. This point could be met by saying that one perceived sounds or smells, but I doubt if holders of the theory want to say this. A more important objection is that the traditional theories of perception have never considered inspection of the contents of consciousness as sufficient for a satisfactory account of perceiving; in fact their analyses have mainly been based on other considerations, epistemological or physiological, and even the sense-datum theory, which values such inspection, seems to subordinate it to, indeed transform it by, the question: 'What in view of illusions, etc., can I be certain of?' And although I have rejected the arguments for sense-data, I am going to suggest that there are features in the perceptual situation which support a distinction between observing and something which may be called sensing, features which would have to be explained away before it could be agreed that observing is unanalysable.

My case will be based on a methodological principle of wider application, namely that to give a proper account of P perceiving O we must consider not only how this situation appears to the percipient P but also the account external observers would give of it, since to say that P perceives O is to imply an objective publicly verifiable relation between them—after all if O is not acting on his senses he is not perceiving it. Hence the scientific account of the causal

[1] See Firth's article in *Mind* (Oct. 1949 and Jan. 1950).

process so closely bound up with his perceiving O is of vital relevance, and neither it nor the results of psychological experiments on percipients can be left unexplained. Admittedly these external observers have to rely on perception, but this is no objection provided that the usual precautions for scientific accuracy are taken and their evidence is not used to prove a general conclusion from which its falsity would follow. Once one has admitted that other persons besides oneself exist, then failure to use their evidence as to what is occurring while one is perceiving is simply to ignore relevant facts—a course which at best causes unnecessary labour and at worst leads to absurdity. Indeed philosophers do use other people's evidence when it suits them, e.g., evidence about *delirium tremens* which it is charitable to suppose they have not had themselves; so why not use it throughout? Why listen to the drunkard but not to the physiologist? Others may mis-perceive as may you, but the well-known procedures for gaining perceptual assurance are speeded if co-operative, and even if they 'go it alone', philosophers do eventually reach perceptual assurance; but having thus validated the perception on which physiologists and psychologists must ultimately rely, they must then consider the problems which the scientific evidence notoriously produces.

If we admit this evidence then there seem to be two main arguments which can be adduced to support a distinction between observing and a basic form of sensing: the first is that interpretation or similar activity occurs in perception, and there must then be something interpreted, i.e., sensations; the second is from physiology and is too often little more than the bare assertion that a sensation corresponds to every excitation of the sensory areas of the brain. In view of the difficulty of distinguishing such sensations the arguments must be amplified and improved; I shall try to state them as plausibly as I can, which will involve some departure from the usual language and theoretical corollaries.

In the first argument 'interpretation' is a traditional term which is not very satisfactory since it suggests that the activities concerned are intellectual; some indeed do seem to involve awareness of meaning, but they range down to normally automatic adjustments which can apparently be achieved by birds or even fish. Perhaps 'modification' or 'organization' would do, but no term is really adequate. The argument is chiefly concerned with sight, since that is the sense in which sensations are most difficult, if not impossible, to discover by inspection. In many discussions reference is made to 'the Stimulus', but as this can be confusing I shall refer here to 'theoretical properties', meaning those properties which from the nature of the object and the laws of perspective and optics it is estimated the object should seem to have, and which can be confirmed by substituting a camera or other instrument for the observer. The core of the argument is that although the theoretical properties vary closely with changes in the object or its position or lighting, yet the perceived qualities of the object, i.e., how it actually looks to a normal percipient or what is noticed of it, do not show a consonant variation. Often these perceived qualities vary when the object and its theoretical properties do not, as in recognition and attention, and sometimes the converse is true as in object constancy. This discrepancy is then explained as due to the modification (selection, interpretation or adjustment) by the percipient of a basic awareness or sensing, the content of which corresponds to the theoretical properties, provided that his sense organs are not defective, though even then a similar modification occurs. This basic sensing may be closely approached or even attained in certain circumstances, but it and the modifying of it must normally be regarded as unconscious activities postulated to account for the discrepancy. To take a few examples; when we attend closely to an object we notice patches of light and shade or shadows of unexpected hue, details which have to be discerned and painted by the artist in order to get realism, and which appear in a photograph; it thus seems that though they are not normally noticed they are 'there all the time', i.e., are always part of the content of the postulated sensing, and that without them we would not see things with their normal shape, depth and colour. Furthermore a great deal of our perceiving is cursory or selective. From photographs, closer observation and similar evidence it is clear that we frequently fail to observe quite gross features of an object, whether through inattention or limited interest or a concentration on its meaning—a hoary example being that of the difference between normal and proof reading of the same passage, though this kind of inattention is widespread in ordinary life. On reflection we feel that we have been influenced by and selected from all the available details, but quite unconsciously. Could this occur without some unconscious analogue of awareness of them? Again recognition may have a noticeable effect on how a thing looks to us. In puzzle photographs of things from unusual angles we at first seem to see a group of shapes and then suddenly recognize the object, after which it stands out in a special way; this sort of change may also occur when we look for and suddenly notice an animal blending with its natural background. Other notorious examples are the reversals, e.g., the staircase figure or the drawing that looks now a goblet, now two faces; perceptual consciousness changes involuntarily but the drawing does not. For the converse there is object constancy in many properties. It is easiest to illustrate in shape: the famous round penny still looks round or nearly so when seen on the table and at an angle not too far from the vertical; but if the background is cut off by a screen or by looking down a tube the penny looks quite elliptical from the same angle. Its theoretical properties,[1] and so the supposed sensing, correspond to the latter appearance in both cases, but in the normal situation unconscious adjustments of perception make it look more nearly round.

The argument then concludes that in sight there is a basic sensing which is normally overlaid by interpretations and adjustments, but which can be attained by a special effort of attention aided by devices like reduction screens. This conclusion may be extended to the other senses also: some at least of the modifying factors seem discoverable in hearing, for example attention and recognition. We can listen to the news without noticing anything about the quality of the announcer's voice, or learn to recognize different instruments in what to the untutored is a confused orchestral sound. But such considerations are not so important in these other senses, for it seems easier to distinguish between the sound or smell and the interpretation of it.

It is not easy to assess this argument exactly. The main weakness is that it seems to indicate two modes of awareness as sensing, and one cannot accept the suggestion that they are identical. The awareness reached by the special effort of attention required by painters, 'perceptual reduction' as it has been called, cannot be identified simply with the postulated basic sensing underlying all these modifications, even assuming that object constancy and the rest can all be removed at once; for this reduction seems to involve a careful scanning, focusing each part of the object in turn on the most sensitive part of the retina, whereas it is dubious to what extent this is done in normal perceiving. Thus the content of the supposed sensing will

[1] This type of interpretation of object constancy is controversial in that some maintained that the constancy adjustment is a purely physiological one, so that if the screens were not there the object as sensed would have the perceived rather than the theoretical qualities. It is difficult to see how there could be a purely physiological adjustment for shape, and such an explanation is chiefly advanced for colour and brightness constancy; but even then there is evidence that the adjustment is learned and that individuals can train themselves to see the theoretical rather than the normally perceived brightness (or even in some cases *vice versa*). See Woodworth, *Experimental Psychology*, pp. 621 and 603.

hardly be so well-defined. However this requires the qualification rather than the rejection of the theory, which will have to say that perceptual reduction reveals a form of awareness which, though less sharply defined, is generally similar to the postulated sensing. And since these phenomena of attention, recognition, etc., are so extraordinarily pervasive and cannot be left unaccounted for, I am inclined to accept the suggestion that they be co-ordinated and explained by postulating normally unconscious interpretations and adjustments of a basic sensing within perceiving; reflection or experiment can reveal these modifying factors, but we can perhaps only approach thereby the basic sensing without quite attaining it. Some may feel that the cure is worse than the disease, but we are fairly used to explanations by unconscious wishes; unconscious sensings or sensations are no worse, and are likewise felt to be of value to psychologists; and the sceptics are faced with a serious disease—how without assuming some sort of unconscious awareness can they explain reading for example, where we may be so absorbed as not at the time to seem sensuously aware of anything? The explanation of the unconscious mental activities themselves is part of the larger mind/body problem, of which I can say no more here than that I suspect they are really unconscious brain activity, i.e., brain activity of the same general type as that which occurs in conscious wishes and sensings (and so describable as such in lieu of adequate physiological descriptions), but lacking in some as yet unknown characteristic responsible for consciousness.

We must note, however, that if we accept such a postulated basic sensing, it cannot, on this argument, be regarded as an adverbial 'having sensations' or as awareness of private existents; that will require the physiological argument if it can be shown at all. So far the basic sensing may be a kind of awareness of the public theoretical characteristics of physical objects, and that it is this and not just having sensations is prima facie supported by the use of cameras to reproduce a two-dimensional version of these properties, and by the repetition by various persons of the experiments concerned.

The physiological argument might run: in perception light rays, sound waves, etc., from the object strike the sense organ, as the result of which nervous impulses travel to the brain and cause activity in it. It is immaterial here whether we then say that this activity causes sensations which with interpretations become perceptual consciousness, or that it causes further brain activity, the whole complex of brain activity being on a double aspect theory identical with per-

ceptual consciousness; the point is that, however caused or related to
brain activity, this consciousness would presumably occur if the
same brain activity were caused in a different way, for example wholly
internally; thus when and only when physiology is taken into account
it may be concluded that perceptual consciousness is really adverbial,
a mode of experiencing and internal activity normally but not
necessarily due to the appropriate external object, although it does
not seem adverbial to the percipient. This is supported by the fact
that mental imagery, especially in dreams and hallucinations, may be
subjectively similar to perceiving; in such cases there is activity in the
nervous system similar to that in genuine perceiving, but as there is
no appropriate external object or cause the imagery is more plausibly
adverbial.

A divergence of view now seems possible as we have to explain why
an adverbial experience is perceptual consciousness, though not
always perception, of an external object. The usual way would be to
postulate a more pervasive interpretation of a more basic sensation,
supposing that without this unconscious 'projection' the sensations
caused by brain activity would seem to be simply a mode of experiencing or rather at such an elementary level would not seem
either adverbial or external. Since we never experience such sensations
we should then have to postulate them as an ideal limit to the
process of stripping off the interpretations and modifications involved
in perceiving, a process which cannot be fully achieved. Another
way would be to set the limit of this process nearer to perceiving and
say that in our experience pains, tickles and similar bodily sensations
are almost always roughly located, e.g., one has not just a pain but
a pain in the leg, and this may be an essential feature of sensations
not originating in the brain, due to the fact that with different
sensations different sensory areas are activated; so an apparent externality, or at least a placing at the sense organ, might be an essential
feature of the content of visual, auditory and similar sensing, since it
is caused by nerve impulses from externally activated sense organs.
For the first view it could be said that misplacing of pains occurs, as in
referred pains, which suggests misinterpretation, while against this
could be argued the impossibility of surmounting such illusions. In
such a speculative matter it is difficult to make a decision; I am
inclined to favour the second view as it has to draw a smaller cheque on
the unconscious, but perhaps something of both is required.

On either view sensing is postulated as an experience which is
immediately caused by (or identical with) the excitation of the sensory

areas of the brain as a result of impulses from the sense organs, and which is converted into perceptual consciousness by various modifications presumably involving further brain activity. The content of sensing on the second view agrees fairly well with that supposed by the argument from interpretation, on which colours, sounds and so on will still seem external, though not identified as properties of this or that physical object; but if one wished to maintain the more usual first view one could still hold that there was some interpretation involved in this apparent externality, though the same would have to be said about the location of pains.

So far we have diverged a little from the ordinary form of the physiological argument by allowing the possibility that sensing, if it could be experienced, might not seem an adverbial mode of experience or a having of sensations like bodily feelings or pains, but might seem awareness of something external. But a more radical break with the common account is needed in two important respects. First, it is only *qua* outside observer that one has any definite evidence for saying that sensing is adverbial, and this is equally true of perceptual consciousness. From this external point of view both are adverbial in being experiences normally caused by external objects but capable of occurring if the appropriate brain activity is otherwise caused; but since from this point of view awareness of an external object is identical with having this experience caused by the object's affecting the sense organs, they are in a perceptual situation both equally forms of awareness of external objects, though differing in content. Also if, as is suggested by the argument from interpretation, we conceive of perceiving or observing as a gradation of various degrees of modification and adjustment, with sensing as the lower limit to the scale, then some experiences, e.g., of unidentified sounds,[1] will be very low down on the scale, though with probably enough locating or discernment from background involved to put them within perceiving. The existence of such marginal cases does not affect the general distinction between observing and sensing, but it does underline the point being made here, namely that there is no ground in the argument for saying that the two activities differ in being one, the awareness of something external and the other, merely adverbial, merely a mode of experiencing. It is therefore inadvisable to refer to

[1] Our original provisional definition of observing or perceiving should be widened so as to allow its object to be any public thing or event, even a sound or smell. This might have seemed question-begging at first, but should be acceptable now that it appears that the difference we seek is one in mode of apprehension not in type of object.

this basic sensing as 'having sensations' since the contrast between sensation proper (pains, itches, etc.) and observation suggests this erroneous distinction.

Secondly we must scrupulously avoid the common story that in sensing the person is aware of ideas, images or sensations, and then in perceiving is conscious of a private world built up out of them. This view is illustrated by analogies of the Lockian type, only with the progress of science the king in his presence room is supplanted by the man in the telephone exchange or the housemaid watching bell indicators in the kitchen. However it is notoriously self-refuting in that if perceiving is thus of a private world the evidence for its causation by public objects, which suggested this, is thereby nullified. This error can be avoided if we realise that, on the physiological evidence and from the external point of view implied by it, what perceiving an object means is having an experience caused by that object's acting on the sense organs; hence we cannot perceive ideas, sensations or private worlds, nor can we be conscious or aware of them if, as often in perceptual contexts, those terms are being used as synonyms of perceive.

To sum up then. We have rejected the sense-datum accounts of sensing; it cannot be regarded as awareness of a private object, or as a purely adverbial experience which is not at the same time awareness of a public external object, or as part of an alternative language without theoretical implications. But, purely as an explanatory hypothesis in order to account for a number of perceptual phenomena, one may postulate a basic sensing which is distinguished from perceiving or observing in the following ways: though we are never conscious of it as such, sensing is a postulated constant element within observing, which is in turn regarded as the result of modifying the sensing by various interpretations and adjustments, which differ in degree and complexity on different occasions; the content of sensing (i.e., how an external object looks or sounds when sensed) will be, it is supposed, a less well-defined version of the colour expanses, patches of light and shade, sounds of a certain tone and so on, which one can be aware of in perceptual reduction aided by devices like reduction screens; thus the effort of attention made in detailed phenomenological investigations can enable us to approach, but probably not reach, the basic sensing. There is, however, no ground for making a further distinction, that such sensing is adverbial, a having of sensations, while observing is awareness of external objects. Such a distinction could only be made from the point of view of an external investigator, not by inspection of perceptual consciousness, and from such an external point of view both are equally forms of awareness of public objects and types of experience caused by such objects, since on the physiological evidence these two descriptions mean the same in this context.

2. RICHARD WOLLHEIM

Mr. Hirst is surely right when he points out that the distinction between sensing and observing is only one of many similar distinctions drawn by philosophers of the present and past alike, all with a single purpose: that of marking off a higher, less fundamental mode, manner, form of perception from one that is lower, more fundamental, basic perhaps. In this way it takes its place along with such other distinctions as those between hard data and soft data, between direct awareness and indirect awareness, between seeing directly and seeing indirectly, between seeing ideas and seeing things, between having sense-data and perceiving material objects. This being so, there is at least a prima facie case for saying that before we can understand what is peculiar to any one of these distinctions, we must first know what is common to them all: on the grounds that all being different answers to a single question, all different versions of a single enterprise, we must first learn what this question, what this enterprise may be. Such at any rate is Mr. Hirst's method, and in this paper I shall follow him: that is to say, in considering the difference between sensing and observing, I shall attend more to the spirit than to the letter of the distinction.

I

But though the problem that lies at the heart of our discussion is an ancient one, it has of recent years encountered certain vicissitudes, of a sort that are indeed recurrent in the history of philosophy. For it is a marked feature in the lives of the great traditional problems that they are from time to time subjected to certain radical proposals of method; which, though they may in the eyes of some transform them out of all recognition, also rejuvenate them and ensure their continued existence. What to the more conservative seem like symptoms of death are in fact earnests of longevity.

Of those recent proposals which have been made in connexion with our problem, Mr. Hirst has something to say on two. As I cannot agree with what he says on either, I will consider each of them in turn. The first is that the distinction between sensing and observing be seen in terms of the distinction between two languages, i.e. the sense-datum language and the material-object language: the second that it be seen in terms of the distinction between tasks and achievements.

A. Mr. Hirst is very sharp with those philosophers who put forward the first proposal. But, as I see it, his sharpness is in large measure misdirected, arising as it does out of a misconception of what it is that they propose. For what he does is to confound *the general proposal* which they do make, a proposal about what question is to be asked—namely, what is the relationship between two different levels of language—with *one particular proposal* that could be made in answer to this question—namely, that the relationship is one of mutual entailment. In other words, he assimilates all forms of linguistic epistemology to the most rigorous and thoroughgoing phenomenalism. Convinced—rightly, to my mind—of the sins of the latter, he tries to visit them on the heads of the former.

But, of course, the assimilation on which this argument depends is quite invalid. For to any question there can in principle be more than one answer: so to propose a question can never be to impose an answer. I do not know why Mr. Hirst makes this confusion, but I can see various possible reasons. One is the historical fact that most philosophers who have raised the particular question have answered it in the way that Mr. Hirst has come to think of as the only way. Another is the widespread feeling that though 'p entails and/or is entailed by q' is an informative answer to the question 'What is the relation between p and q?', 'p neither entails nor is entailed by q' is not; so in the cases where the latter answer is the correct one, it is felt that the question is a fruitless one to raise. But this would be so only if all we could say about the relationship between various sentences is whether they do or do not entail one another. And surely—as I shall try to exhibit in this paper—we can say more. A third possible reason for Mr. Hirst's confusion is that he is misled by his own expression: 'the alternative language theory'. For this expression could be used to mean *both* the theory that there are two 'alternative' (in the sense of 'different') sensory languages whose relationship is an open question *and also* the theory that these languages are 'alternatives' in the sense of equivalent and so interchangeable.

Furthermore, though I agree with Mr. Hirst in rejecting a thoroughgoing phenomenalism, according to which there are equivalences holding between one level of language and the other, I cannot accept his reasons for doing so. For surely it is no serious objection to say, as he does, that if the equivalences asserted hold only between *simple* material-object sentences and *composite* sense-datum sentences—as, on any plausible version of the theory, they must—then this 'would weaken the claim to neatness'. For no phenomenalist has ever claimed for his theory neatness of this puritanical kind. And again, it is not conclusive to argue that since perceiving 'is more than just having sensory experiences and involves some non-sensory activity', therefore 'statements solely about sensings, even a group of them, cannot be equivalent to a statement about observing, since they cannot do justice to its non-sensory element'. For why should not this non-sensory element or element of interpretation in observing, consist in supplying all the sensory sentences other than the one that refers to the current sensing? I do not myself think that this is a correct view but if it is to be dismissed it must first be disproved.

Mr. Hirst has however some further arguments against a linguistic treatment of the problem of perception, which do not rely on the assumption that any such treatment must be phenomenalistic. What they amount to is a charge of disingenuousness. According to him, no purely linguistic treatment is possible: so-called linguistic philosophers attest to this in their practice, if not in their preaching: for their theories always contain some factual reference or supposition.

But Mr. Hirst's argument here I find unclear, because I am not sure what he means by 'sense-datum theory'. At times he seems to mean by it what is otherwise called 'sense-datum language'. Then presumably his argument is that any version of such a language must refer to fact. But this is of course what no linguistic philosopher would wish or seek to deny. Or perhaps his argument is that any version of such a language must refer not merely to fact but to fact not referred to in the material-object language. But again, this is not damaging to the thesis that we should attend to the relationship between the two languages: on the contrary, it is merely another way of saying that this relationship is not one of mutual entailment.

But Mr. Hirst seems also to use the expression 'sense-datum theory' to mean not the sense-datum language but the assertion that there is such a language. Then his argument would be that to make such an assertion is always to make, implicitly perhaps, an assertion about the existence of certain facts: and the facts that he seems to have in mind are the facts to which the sense-datum language refers. But this is a mistake. For to assert that a certain language exists is not to assert or to suppose that the facts to which it refers exist, but to assert that they could exist. And this—in the relevant sense of the word 'fact'—is not an assertion or supposition of fact at all.[1]

So much for Mr. Hirst's charges against linguistic epistemology. It might reasonably be expected that I should for my part produce arguments in its favour. But I do not intend to. For it seems to me that discussions about the *value* of various philosophical methods—as opposed, that is, to discussions of their *possibility*—are barren affairs when conducted in abstract terms. With such puddings at least, the proof is in the eating.

B. But though Mr. Hirst may be excessively sceptical of the benefits of any linguistic approach to this problem, he seems to me excessively optimistic about the application to it of Professor Ryle's distinction between tasks and achievements. (And in a way this is paradoxical: for surely the latter is just an instance of the former?)

Mr. Hirst thinks that he can explain, in terms of this distinction, the fact that 'I see x' (and 'I observe x' in the requisite sense of 'observe') entails 'x exists'. For once we recognize that 'see' is (and 'observe' can be) an achievement-word, then we can account for the existence of x in all cases of seeing and observing by regarding it as that extra condition, over and above the conditions involved in the performance of the subsidiary task, that is always present when the use of an achievement-word is justified. But the argument is lame. For if we turn to the relevant task-words such as 'look at', or 'watch', or 'observe' (in the other sense), we shall see that their use also involves the existence of their objects. This is not apparent from *The Concept of Mind* because Professor Ryle takes as the relevant task-words verbs such as 'try to make out'[2] or 'search'[3] (presumably 'search for') or 'scan'[4] (presumably 'scan something for'). Now, it is true that these verbs, unlike 'see', do not entail the existence of their objects. And it is true that these verbs *also* stand to 'see' (and 'observe' in the appropriate sense) in the relation of task-words to achievement-words. But they are not the task-words that are relevant to the present

---

[1] In fairness to Mr. Hirst, it must be pointed out that this confusion in the usage of the expression 'sense-datum theory' is not peculiar to him but derives indeed from the writings of the sense-datum philosophers themselves, e.g. A. J. Ayer, *The Foundations of Empirical Knowledge*, where all theories of perception are regarded not, as one might expect, as so many theories about languages but as so many languages. One reason for this is a failure to distinguish between implications and entailments: so that e.g. 'If I see an x, I see a sense-datum of an x'—which is part of a language—is made to do duty for 'I see an x' entails 'I see a sense-datum of an x' which is part of a theory about a language.

[2] *The Concept of Mind*, p. 223.

[3] Ibid. p. 303.

[4] Ibid. p. 238.

argument since they do not designate tasks of any epistemological interest. Therefore the fact that they do not entail the existence of their objects proves nothing: whereas the fact that verbs such as 'watch' do entail the existence of their objects, proves much.[1]

Further, I cannot see that the fact that 'I see x' entails 'x exists' requires explanation. For surely nearly all transitive verbs have precisely this entailment. It is those that do not—and a miscellaneous collection they are—that seem to stand in need of some comment: verbs, that is to say, as divergent as 'imagine', and 'hunt', and 'fear'.

And, finally, I cannot see that this entailment has quite the significance for our problem that is claimed for it in *The Concept of Mind*. For there it is argued that those sense-datum philosophers who attributed incorrigibility to sensory statements came to do so as a result of transferring the existence-commitment from a higher-order achievement word to a lower order task-word. But this diagnosis is unconvincing. For surely the temptation to ascribe incorrigibility to sensory statements arises at an earlier state in their argument. Let us set out a typical sense-datum thesis schematically as follows:—e.g.

'I seem to see (sense 1) a red patch' entails 'I see (sense 2) a red sense-datum' entails 'A red sense-datum exists'.

And here we see that it could not be the second move in this argument, but it might be the first that gives rise to the incorrigibility thesis. It *could not* be the second, because here the sensory statement to which incorrigibility is supposed to attach figures as the antecedent and not as the consequent in the argument. But it *might be* the first, because here the sensory statement does appear as the consequent: and as the consequent to a statement that, on one interpretation at least, might well seem incorrigible. For sometimes 'I seem to see a red patch' is interpreted as 'I think I see a red patch'. And if this statement is incorrigible, then so is the sensory statement: for presumably the consequent of any incorrigible statement must itself be incorrigible.

II

I conceive then the general problem of sensing and observing to be

[1] It is significant that Ryle actually quotes perceptual task verbs that in fact do entail the existence of their objects, though without recognizing this. So, for instance, he mentions 'watch' (p. 303) or 'scrutinize' (ibid): and in doing so, provides ammunition against himself.

that of the relationship between the sensory language and the material-object language. As such, it is vast in scope, and in the rest of this paper I shall touch on only two or three aspects of it and make no claim to exhaustiveness: but as these aspects are of major importance, my treatment even of them may well be found cursory.

What is meant by 'the material-object language' I shall, following current philosophical practice, assume to hold no particular difficulties: it is the language that we ordinarily use to talk of watching and perceiving material objects. But the nature of 'the sensory language' is not so clear. And yet that there is a problem here to perplex us is surely revealing. For it is odd to think that we might be worried in this same way about the German language or the Hebrew language, not knowing what they really were. Or if we were, our minds could be so easily set at rest. We should be told that the language in question was 'the language spoken by such-and-such people' or 'the language spoken in such and-such a place' or 'the language that is the modern descendant of such-and-such a language'.

Now, the sensory language clearly has no such secondary characteristics. And this might be the reason why we cannot settle what it really is. But surely it isn't: for even if it did have such characteristics, we should not as philosophers use them to refer to it. For our interest as philosophers in a given expression of language is not merely, as some have thought, in such logical characteristics as it possesses, but, more particularly, in such logical characteristics as it *necessarily* possesses. But we can only say that something necessarily possesses certain logical characteristics when we have referred to it or picked it out by certain other logical characteristics.

From this it follows that even if there were secondary characteristics that the sensory language was commonly said to possess, we could not, as philosophers, use them to refer to it: for we ought not to refer to it by any secondary characteristics at all. But neither could we use such logical characteristics as it might commonly be said to possess. For even if common usage can never be wrong in its logic, it may be—and often is—wrong in the characterization of its logic.

So if we are, as philosophers, to discuss the sensory language, we shall have to characterize for ourselves its logical features as succinctly and as unmistakably as possible. It is though important to see *why* we must do this, and how, contrary to what is often said, it has nothing to do with the question of the existence or otherwise of a sensory language within one or more of the natural languages. Confusion on this point often creeps into philosophical discussion about the necessity or otherwise of the creation of a sensory language. What is necessary is to create the specification of the language, not the language itself: and so whether the language already exists or not is irrelevant.

Now all hitherto existing attempts—and I should like to say unreservedly *all* attempts—to characterize the sensory language follow one or other of two general methods which I shall consider in turn:

1. The first method—which might be called the indirect method—is that of introducing the sensory language by reference to, or as a derivation from, the material-object language. There are various arguments of this kind, most of them making use of an example. A situation is quoted in which someone claims to see a material object, say, a brown stick. Then an interlocutor is introduced who by pointing out one after another the various dangers that attend the making of such a claim, makes him reduce it, contract it, until he reaches a bare minimum. Or alternatively, while the observer himself is left in the dark about the real situation, we are put in the superior position of knowing that these dangers are in fact realized and that the stick he claimed to see is not brown but red, or is not straight but crooked, or is not a real stick at all but a hallucination or a mirror image: and then we are invited to do for him what, if he had been more cautious, he might have done for himself, and to reduce his claim until it is consistent with the facts.

Doubtless these arguments vary somewhat in detail: but, even then, more in the commentary attached to the moves away from the original claim than in the moves themselves. For these all follow a similar path marked out by such obvious signposts as:

I see a brown stick.
I see what looks like (seems to be) a brown stick.
I see what looks to me like (seems to me to be) a brown stick.

In some cases intermediate steps are inserted into the sequence, and in many cases special technical terms (e.g. 'sense-data', 'sensa') appear in it but as these are avowedly introduced by means of definitions in use they constitute no problem in principle.

Now however these moves or reductions of claims are to be described, what seems clear is that there is a point at which they come to a halt. The terminal claim then is to be considered as a claim in the sensory language: and the sensory language itself as the sum of all sentences used to make any claim of this sort.

2. The second method of introducing the sensory language might

in contrast be called the direct method, for according to it the sensory language is characterized not by reference to some other language, the material-object language, but by reference to that in the world which it is used to describe. So it is spoken of as the language of 'the given', of 'direct awareness', of 'what is immediately perceived'.

Now at first this second method might well seem superior to the other just on account of its directness. But when we come to reflect on it, its advantages no longer appear so bright. For expressions such as 'the given' or 'that of which we are directly aware' come from the vernacular into philosophy with no more than a half-meaning, attended, that is, by indications of what they could mean but by no certain instructions about what they do mean. The philosopher must complete these before he can serviceably use them: and there are two ways open to him of doing this.

One way would be to try and give the meaning of, say, 'the given' by indicating the sort of sentences that can be used to describe or refer to the given. But if the point of elucidating this expression is so that we shall then be able to use it to characterize the notion of a sensory language, any attempt to do so by reference to the sensory language would be too narrowly circular.

The other way would be to try to explicate a notion such as 'the given' in terms of what seem like cognate notions such as 'perception', 'observing a material-object', 'looking at a stick'. But if we consider the way in which we would arrive at the notion of 'the given' by starting from them, how the explication would actually run, we see that such a line of argument would be no more than a meta-linguistic version of the chain of perceptual claims that takes us from the material-object language claim to the sensory language claim. Moreover the movement of the former would not merely be parallel to that of the latter, it would be attendant upon it. For each step that we take in our explication would be determined by, and would itself be fully explicable only in terms of, some claim that we could make in the perceptual language at our disposal.

I may perhaps best explain my meaning by referring to a famous explication of this kind which has already been quoted by Mr. Hirst: that to be found in Price's *Perception*[1]. There we are led to the notion of the given from that of seeing a material object by a consideration of the possibilities of doubt. 'When I see a tomato there is much that I can doubt.' And step by step Price takes us through all the stations of doubt—Mr. Hirst has already enumerated them—until he brings

[1]H. H. Price, *Perception*, p. 3.

us at last to that which we cannot doubt. 'That something is red and round then and there I cannot doubt.' And this, according to Price is the given. But how does Price determine these stations of doubt? How does he know how many there are, and where they are? It seems to me that what he does is to consider the various ways in which we can express our doubts, and then one by one to subtract the doubts that we can express from our original claim. And I do not see what else he could do.

This point, that the direct method of introducing the sensory language is—paradoxical though it may sound—dependent on the indirect method, has considerable bearing on the question whether there is an ultimate sensory language, whether there is a class of claims that we cannot in principle reduce. It has been maintained by many philosophers that there is. And the attempt to introduce the sensory language by the direct method tends to make this thesis seem plausible. For if there really were in experience something that was the given and that was in principle not further analysable, then surely there would be in language certain claims that characterized the given and that were in principle not further reducible.

But if, as we have seen, every stage in the move from the perception of material objects to the given is determined by the perceptual resources of our language, then so is the last stage in the move. And from this it follows that any attempt to characterize the sensory language in terms of the given (or any similar term) uniquely refers, within a natural language, to a specific set of claims when and only when the linguistic resources of that language have been stipulated. For as these resources increase or decrease, so will the reference of the characterization shift. And if this is so, then we must abandon altogether the notion of an absolute sensory language. For clearly there is no *a priori* way in which we can fix for ever the wealth or poverty of a language calculated in perceptual terms. There is no reason why new methods of reducing claims should not be incorporated into it or established methods rejected.

An example may perhaps bring out what I mean. We should ordinarily say, I think, that in English the lowest sort of perceptual claim we could make is one of the form, 'I see what looks to me like a brown stick'. And so we should say that with the English language, claims of this sort constituted the sensory language. But it is not impossible that, at some moment, sense should be given to the expression 'what looks to me to look to me like . . . .' and so to claims such as 'I see what looks to me to look to me like a brown stick' and this would certainly be a lower claim than that above, and so would replace it as the paradigm of the sensory language. Again expressions like the current 'looks to me like' might drop out of the language and there be no means of forming claims lower than 'I see what looks like a brown stick'. And then it would be claims of this sort that we should come to think of as forming the sensory language.

If we accept the fact that there can be no absolute sensory language, there are two ways open to us of looking at the situation. One is to see the sensory language as an ideal, as a limit towards which we can move but which can never be attained. The other—and the more helpful—is this: If we re-write the expression 'sensory language' as a relative superlative, i.e. as equivalent to 'the lowest level language in a given natural language', and then re-write this as an antecedent and a relative clause, the relative clause will be what grammarians call a 'restrictive' (Jespersen) or a 'defining' (Fowler) clause, i.e. the total expression will appear as 'the language that in a given language is of the lowest level'.

The significance of this for our general problem is that the expression 'sensing' can no longer be regarded as the name of some specific activity (either a task or an achievement) which could be further defined or characterized in terms of certain physical descriptions. It is not like 'climbing Mount Everest' or 'looking at the Ansidei Madonna', but like 'climbing the highest mountain in the world' or 'looking at the most beautiful picture in the world' when these are used without any presupposition of geographical fact or aesthetic taste.

For this reason I view with suspicion Mr. Hirst's attempt to arrive at a fuller explication of this expression by reference to the facts of physiology and psychology. More particularly, I do not see why he says that in our analysis of what it is for subject P to observe x, or to sense y, we should 'consider' the evidence of 'external observers' when it is clear that this evidence neither is known by the observer nor follows from what he knows. For if we do consider this evidence to good purpose, if, that is to say, we incorporate it into our analysis, either we shall have to conclude that people very often do not know that they are observing x or sensing y when we should ordinarily say that they do: or else we shall have to rest on a dual analysis of 'P observes x' or 'P senses y', one sort being applicable when the claim is made by P, the other sort applicable when it is made by an external observer. And surely neither can be a satisfactory outcome of a philosophical analysis.

III

So far I have discussed the sensory language in terms of the 'reduction of perceptual claims', while I have left this expression itself
unexplained as though its meaning were clear to all. Possibly I have
this much justification for doing so—that it means something to everyone. But what is necessary for our purpose is that it should mean the
same thing to everyone, otherwise the various arguments in favour
of the sensory language will be in much the same position as the traditional proofs for the existence of God; that is to say, even if they all
established something there would be no reason to believe that what
was established in each case was identical.

Perhaps this notion of reduction—which is, I take it, the converse
of Mr. Hirst's 'interpretation'—can best be approached by contrasting it with various related or cognate activities; in this way we shall
at least arrive at some knowledge of what it is not.

1. In the first place, we may contrast the *reduction* of a claim with
the *correction* of it: the case where the observer contracts his ground
with the case where he shifts it. So, for example, the move from 'I see
a man' to 'I see what looks like a man' would count as an instance of
the first sort: that from 'I see a man' to 'I see a woman' as an instance
of the second. I do not of course wish to deny that there is a sense in
which a reduced claim might be considered a 'correction' of the
original claim in that it might be true where the other was false. But
this is not my usage of the term, and in excluding corrections from
the class of reduced claims I do not wish to reject these cases. What
I wish to provide against are those cases where if the corrected claim
is true, the original claim *must be false*. In other words, a claim and its
reduced claim can never be contradictories.

2. Next, we must distinguish between the reduction of a perceptual
claim, which is the making of a smaller claim about what was seen,
and the making of a claim about seeing something smaller. For the
moment, one example will suffice. The move from 'I saw a tree' to
'I saw what looked like a tree' is one sort of move: that from 'I saw
a tree' to 'I saw a branch of the tree' is a plausible— though, as we shall
see, not a necessary—example of the other.

3. Finally, we can, I think distinguish between reducing a claim
and asserting the claim more tentatively or less emphatically. There
are various ways in which we can, as it were, 'mute' a claim that we
have made: either by the tone of voice or by prefacing it with expressions such as 'possibly', 'perhaps', 'I think that . . . . . ' I must confess

though that I am not altogether clear on this point, nor entirely certain whether such moves should be marked off from reductions proper. On the whole I think that they should be, because I think that the resultant claim is not properly a perceptual claim. For if we ask what it is on such occasions that we claim to see, the answer is some such expression as 'possibly a stick', 'what I think is an orange', and these are surely not descriptions of what is seen, perceptual descriptions: they could not, for instance, be illustrated, or be taught in visual situations.

However the fact that these various processes can be readily characterized does not mean that in practice they can be easily identified or that genuine cases of reduction can always be marked off from those that are not. Perhaps though a consideration of these border-line cases might help us to a better understanding of the distinctions themselves.

1. First of all, let us take the distinction between the reduction and the correction of a claim: and consider the case of the move from 'I see a man' to 'I see a man or a woman'. The reason we should have for saying that this is a case of reduction rather than of correction is clear enough. Our criterion gives an unambiguous answer. And yet if we suppose this move to be made as the first stage in the move from 'I saw a man' to 'I saw a woman', and if we further suppose that the observer had at the time of making it made up his mind that what he saw was a woman, there seems good reason for our classifying it as one of correction. If, however, we follow this suggestion, we shall find that it leads us into taking a much broader view of the way in which we are to classify the various cases: for it will mean that we shall have to take into account many features of the situation, e.g. the motive of the observer, that we had previously tended to discount. And this may well be a route that we have no desire to pursue if it can possibly be avoided.

2. Let us take now the distinction between the making of a smaller claim about what was seen and the making of a claim about seeing something smaller. A philosophically interesting case here is that made famous by Moore: that is, the move from 'I see an orange' to 'I see the surface of an orange'. Now an obvious reason for classifying this as not a case of reduction would be that the surface of an orange—however we understand this expression—is clearly something smaller than the whole orange: it stands to it, in fact, in the relation of part to whole. And arguments of this sort have been levelled against Moore and his attempts to introduce sense-data in

terms of this move. On the other hand, it could be urged that though the surface of the orange is indeed smaller than the orange itself, the person in claiming to see it is not claiming to see any less than he did when he claimed to see the orange: for when he claimed to see the orange, he never intended to claim that he saw any more of it than its surface. But then this argument also can go too far. For let us take the move that I quoted earlier as the very paradigm of a move from a claim to see something to a claim to see something less: that from 'I see a tree' to 'I see the branch of a tree'. Could not this move be made by a man who never had seen more of the tree than its branch 'and had never intended to claim that he had? And if so, should we not have to admit that this move, in this context, was a case of reduction? Even here though the issue is not clear. On the one side it could be said that the argument in favour of seeing this move as a reduction was little better than a pun on the word 'intend'. For the man who in claiming to see the orange didn't intend to claim that he saw more of it than its surface, didn't intend to do so because the meaning of the words that he used would not have allowed him to: whereas if the man who claimed to see the tree didn't intend to claim that he saw more of it than a branch, this is not because of what the words mean but because of what he had in mind. And yet, on the other side, it could be countered that the observer in making the claim about the larger object ('the tree') and in intending one only about the smaller object ('the branch of the tree') was not being at all exaggerative or imprecise, and that therefore there is no need for the argument about his intentions to convert the one into the other. We only think there is, because we think that a material object word like 'tree' is always equivalent to 'the whole tree'. But this equivalence though holding in some contexts does not hold in all contexts. 'I saw the tree' does not stand to 'I saw the branch of the tree', as 'I cut down the tree' does to 'I cut down the branch of the tree'.

3. Finally let us turn to the third distinction that I made, that between the reduction of a claim and the less emphatic assertion of it. And here an important case is provided by the two expressions that I have quoted as being of supreme importance in the reduction of claims: 'looks like' and 'seems to be'. For both of these have a use in which they are more or less equivalent to 'what I took to be' or 'what is probably . . . .' Here of course we do not so much have a borderline case as an ambiguous one, a case of a word of more than one meaning: so that if the various senses are carefully kept apart no difficulties need arise.

The difficulties, however, of ascertaining what is a genuine case of reduction and what is not, are not so dangerous as one might think. For in the first place, to think that a case that is not one of reduction is one of reduction, and to pursue it, is more likely to introduce gratuitous slips into our course than to lead us astray. And again, to overlook a case of reduction will not necessarily impair our epistemology for not all reductions are of great philosophic importance. It is only a few that are and they are generally selected for special discussion: those, that is, where the claim is reduced by dropping some major condition, such as that of reality in favour of mere appearance or that of publicity in favour of mere privacy.

IV

So far the discussion of the reduction of claims has been entirely negative. And of course there is in principle nothing defective with this method. We might eventually arrive at a tolerably precise notion of what reduction is after an extensive examination of what it is not. But as many philosophers have claimed to know of a positive condition of reduction, it would be wanton not to consider their argument.

This argument is to the effect that a necessary though clearly not a sufficient condition for reduction is that the lower claim should be entailed by the higher claim. And on the face of it this seems a reasonable suggestion. We have only to consider cases where an observer withdraws from, say, 'I see a stick' to 'I see what looks like a stick' to feel its plausibility, and so to regard expressions such as 'what looks like' as devices to insure the mechanical or necessary character of such moves.

But if we take one of these expressions and examine it, we shall see not only that such entailments do not hold but that they could not hold. Even by making adjustments in our perceptual vocabulary, we could not achieve such a relation between higher and lower claims. The expression I shall consider is 'looks like'.

Now one way in which this expression may be used I have already mentioned, and have argued that this has no connexion with the process of reduction. The expression can however be used as what, in contradistinction, may be called a "perceptual description", and it is in this role that it has attracted the attention of epistemologists— although they have failed to recognize even within this usage a further diversity of usage.

For sometimes when we say that we see what looks like a particular object, we mean that we see what looks like what that object looks like *under normal conditions*, i.e., in good light, in frontal perspective, from no great distance, etc.: in other words, what we see might serve as an illustration of that object in an encyclopaedia or a child's book. But clearly it is not the case that, whenever we see a particular object, what we see looks like what that object looks like under normal conditions. For it is rare for objects to look like what they look like under normal conditions unless they are actually being looked at under normal conditions: and objects are not only looked at under normal conditions. If then it isn't always true that, whenever we see a particular material object, we also see what looks like that material object, *a fortiori* the claim to see a material object does not entail the claim to see what looks like that material object.

However there is another sense in which the expression 'what looks like an x' can be used and still be what I have called 'a perceptual description'. And this is the sense in which to say under certain conditions that one sees what looks like a particular material object is to say that one sees what looks like what that object looks like *under just those conditions*. To see in the twilight or from the top of a steeple what looks like a cow is to see what looks like what a cow ordinarily looks like in the twilight or from the top of a steeple. (And so though 'what looks like an x' is still a perceptual description, it is an incomplete one, requiring the context to fill it out). But though it is true that under any conditions an object is more likely to look like what it ordinarily looks like in those conditions than to look like what it looks like under normal conditions—save, of course, in the limiting case where the actual conditions are the normal conditions and here the two limbs of the comparison become identical—yet there is no logical certainty that it will. So even in this sense of 'looks like', it need not always be true that when we see a material object we see what looks like a material object of that sort; and therefore *a fortiori* the entailment doesn't hold.

But these arguments which show why 'I see x' does not entail 'I see what looks like x', also show more. For they show that whatever perceptual description we insert into our reduced claim, it still will not be entailed by the original claim. For when we observe a material object, there are no sensations that we can be logically certain will occur; and therefore when we assert a material object claim, there are no sensory descriptions that we can be certain will be applicable.

However at this stage it might be countered that, though indeed none of the specific entailments holds, there is a general entailment that does hold: that, though from the truth of a material-object claim the truth of no particular sensory claim follows, the truth of some sensory claim does follow. To put it in the technical language in which it is usually expressed, we might say that though 'I see a stick' does not entail 'I see a' or 'I see b' or 'I see c' where a, b and c are particular kinds of sense-data, it does entail '(Fx) I see x', where the variable ranges over all sense-data.

Prima facie this entailment seems plausible. What inclines me to doubt it is consideration of the hypothetical case of an observer who claims to see some material object, but genuinely finds himself unable to make a reduced claim about what he sees. He can say what it *is* that he sees but not what it *looks like to him*. And we are to believe that his inability springs not from any ignorance of the language, not from any defect of intelligence, but simply from the sense that he would have no good reason for making such a claim. To some, such a situation might seem impossible. To me this is not clearly so, and if we admit its possibility, then I think that there are difficulties in the way of saying that in this case there is a true sensory claim that the man could make. For

1. It seems that there is no possible method for determining what this claim might be. But to some this objection might seem too naïvely positivistic, taken up, as it is, with questions of verification: and the situation might be compared to that of a man playing patience by himself who yesterday turned up a card and failed to observe it. For though we cannot at this moment of time tell which card it was that he turned up, it is yet true that some card was turned up: and the true description of the card that was turned up is the description of the card that was in fact turned up. Similarly the true particular claim is the claim that described what things did in fact look like to him.

2. But, it might be countered, if it is true that, just as sometimes cards are turned up at patience and we know what they are and sometimes cards are turned up and we don't know what they are, so sometimes things look like such-and-such to us and we know what they look like to us and sometimes they look like such-and-such to us and we don't know what they look like to us, then what is *the difference* between the one sort of occasion and the other such that on the one we know and on the other we don't? In the case of the card played at patience, the difference between the two sorts of occasion is clear: for though on both occasions we have turned up a card, on one

occasion we have also noticed what it is and on the other we haven't noticed what it is. But if the analogy between the two cases is a good one, we ought to be able to carry the distinction from the one over to the other. But of course we cannot: or at least cannot without equivocation. For though we can say not only 'I noticed that I played the King of Spades' or 'I noticed what card I played' but also 'I noticed that it looked to me like a duck' or 'I noticed what it looked like to me', the analysis is different for the two sets of expression. For while the first set easily becomes 'I played the King of Spades *and* I noticed this' or 'I played a card *and* I noticed which', the second set resists the parallel analysis into genuine conjunctions such as 'It looked to me like a duck *and* I noticed this' or 'It looked to me like something or other *and* I noticed what'. For these would be pleonastic. The absurdity of this analysis of 'noticing' statements on the assumption that they are genuine conjunctions, is brought out even more vividly if we consider their negations: for then we should have to admit that the negation of 'I noticed that it looked to me like a duck' gives either 'It didn't look to me like a duck and I noticed this' or 'It looked to me like a duck and I didn't notice this' or 'It didn't look to me like a duck and I didn't notice this'. And whereas the first is merely pleonastic, the second and third are absurd.

The reason for this is that noticing is intimately connected with the fact that something looks like such and such to me, whereas it is not so connected with the fact that I played a certain card; it is a condition of the former though certainly not a condition of the latter.

A final point. It might well be asked at this stage if an observer doesn't know how what he sees *looks to him*, how can he know what it *is*? For what other reasons can we have for knowing what we see other than knowing how things look to us? And the answer of course is to be found in our expectations, our habits, the way in which we are primed against experience: the condition, that is, from which the early adherents of Impressionism claimed with understandable vehemence the painting of Monet and Pissarro had come to release us, but which seems more likely to be the average condition of mankind.

And yet if this is so, if a man can legitimately say that he sees something or other and say so as much on the basis of his expectations as on the evidence of his eyes, are we right to call this a case of observation? Is it enough that the sentence he quite correctly uses should be prefaced by some expression such as 'I see' . . . ? Or does this not suggest that the notion of observing has difficulties that remain untouched?

III

THE PROBLEM OF PERCEPTION

ANTHONY QUINTON

I

THE PROBLEM of perception is to give an account of the relationship of sense-experience to material objects. This relationship has traditionally been seen as logical, a matter of showing how beliefs about objects can be established or supported by what we know in immediate experience. For, it is held, only our knowledge of experience is direct, immediate, by acquaintance; what we know or claim to know about objects is indirect, derivative, by inference from what we know directly. Consequently if our beliefs about objects are to have any secure foundation, it must consist in what we know directly, by acquaintance, about sense-data. From this starting-point philosophers have gone on to present varying accounts of the type of inference involved. An extreme view is Hume's, that the passage from experiences to objects rests on 'a kind of fallacy or illusion'. Lockean causal theories assert that the connexion between experiences and objects is contingent and that knowledge of experience is good inductive evidence for beliefs, logically distinct from it, about objects. The species of inference involved is transcendental hypothesis of the type to be found in scientific arguments for the existence of such unobservables as electrons or chromosomes. For phenomenalism the connexion between experiences and objects is necessary, to speak of objects is to speak in an abbreviated way about certain pervasive kinds of regularity in experience. The species of inference involved is simple inductive extrapolation. There are not two worlds, an inner and an outer, but two terminologies. The terminology of objects is used to refer to what is invariant as between the private worlds of experience.

Each view derives strength from the weaknesses of its opponent. The most emphasised weakness of phenomenalism is that, if it were true, unobserved objects would be mere possibilities and actual effects

From *Mind*, Vol. 64 (1955), pp. 28–51. Reprinted by permission of the author and the Editor of *Mind*.

would have to arise from merely potential causes. Mill's view that objects are permanent possibilities of sensation is confronted by a fundamental and unargued incredulity. A more serious difficulty arises about the antecedents of the hypothetical statements which describe the permanent possibilities in question. For these antecedents mention objects. To assume, as phenomenalists often cheerfully do, that these references can be replaced by references to 'orienting experiences' is to beg the very question at issue. One cannot *assume* that statements about experiences are equivalent in meaning to statements about objects in order to *show* that they are. Against the causal theory it is argued that, given the sense-datum theory, it would be impossible ever to know that the logically distinct, unobservable, transcendental causes existed. For a causal inference is only legitimate if it is at least possible to obtain evidence for the existence of the cause which is independent of the events it is held to explain.

In the face of this impasse sense-datum theorists have tended to adopt a middle position of compromise. Causal theorists liken their procedure to the 'model-building' of natural scientists. The external world is a theoretical construction, fruitful and various in its predictive and explanatory consequences. Phenomenalists modify their thesis of the strict logical equivalence of statements about experiences and about objects, in view of the difficulties, in principle and practice, of translating one into the other. Both extremes are abandoned in favour of the view that it is a simple, convenient and fruitful theoretical construction. But this is rather a method of refusing to face the difficulties than of overcoming them. For what sort of theoretical construction is involved, a substantial model of the not-yet-observed like a theory of atomic structure or a mere *façon de parler* like theories of magnetic and gravitational fields?

My purpose in this paper is to overcome these difficulties by a more radical procedure, that of refuting the premise from which both problematic doctrines derive, that we are never directly aware of or acquainted with objects.

My principle target will be the conception of direct awareness or acquaintance itself. The sense-datum theory holds that corresponding to the two kinds of objects of knowledge are two kinds of knowledge—direct and indirect. Thus while no knowledge of material objects is direct, all or only knowledge of experience is direct. In more linguistic terms, while no statements about objects are basic, all or only statements about experience are basic. A piece of knowledge, then, is direct if, and only if, it can be expressed by a basic statement. But this translation is of little help since neither of the crucial terms, 'direct' and 'basic', is clearly intelligible, let alone more intelligible than the other.

Two main kinds of definition are commonly offered of these expressions, one in terms of certainty, the other in terms of inference. By the former I directly know that p (or 'p' is a basic statement) if I know for certain that p. It is held that beliefs about objects are never certain, beliefs about experience are always certain and that for any uncertain belief to be even probable something else must be certain. Consequently all beliefs about objects that are to any extent probable must be logically derived from beliefs about experience. I shall hold that all three of the premises for this conclusion are false. The incorrigibility of statements about experience has been defended, notably by Ayer, on the ground that the only mistakes to which we are liable in making such statements are 'verbal'. I shall attempt to show that this too is false. Sometimes a definition in terms of inference is preferred. I directly know that p (or 'p' is a basic statement) if I know that p without inference. It is not, of course, maintained that in coming to form a belief about an object I undertake any conscious process of reasoning. What is involved is 'implicit' inference. Nevertheless, it is held, reasons exist for beliefs about objects which it is the philosopher's business to render explicit and without reference to which no justification of these beliefs can be provided. I shall argue that there is no relevant sense of 'reason' in which a reason for them always exists.

Why should this have been thought to be so? The sense-datum theory, seemingly a variant of the empiricist principle that all our knowledge of matters of fact is based on sense-experience, tends to assume that principle's authority. But this, like other oracles, owes much of its reputation to ambiguity. It can be taken to assert three different things, two of which are uncontentious while the third deserves close inspection. First, it is an unexciting truth of physiology that sensations, physical stimulations of the sense-organs, are causally necessary conditions of our knowledge of matters of fact. Second, the establishment of any truth about objects logically requires that someone shall have seen, touched or otherwise perceived something. The chains of inference and testimony cannot hang unsupported but must terminate in observation. In this use 'sense-experience' does not mean anything so definite as 'sense-datum', it has no phenomenological flavour. Seeing a tomato is just as much an observation as seeing a round, red, shiny patch. Finally, 'based on sense-experience' can be taken to mean 'logically derived from sense-experience'. The logical derivation in question here is of statements about objects from statements about experiences. It is this third interpretation of the principle that constitutes the sense-datum theory and which I shall attempt to refute.

These definitions of 'direct' and 'basic' in terms of certainty and inference are not, however, the starting-points of sense-datum theories of perception. They are rather conclusions to the argument from illusion in terms of which the expressions 'direct' and 'basic' are normally introduced. This argument holds that objects are not always what they appear to be and that there need be no discoverable difference between two situations in one of which an object is and in the other is not what it appears to be. In consequence, all that we really know is what appears to be the case, since, even when what appears to be the case *is* the case, we cannot there and then tell whether it is or not. Since we know only what appears to be the case, the only things we really perceive are appearances. Some philosophers have protested weakly against the later stages of this argument. I hope to substantiate and fortify their protest.

The mistake lies in the identification of what appears to be the case with our sense-experience. We always know what appears to be the case. So it is appearances, not objects, that we really perceive. But what else are these appearances but our current sense-fields, our sense-experience? The three forms of words; 'this appears to be ϕ', 'there is a ϕ appearance', 'there is a ϕ sense-datum', are held to be equivalent in meaning. I shall argue that a statement of what appears to be the case is rarely a description of our sense-experience and is normally a modified, guarded claim about what *is* the case, expressing an inclination to believe something about objects. The ostensible firmness and incorrigibility of these assertions is a consequence, not of their referring to a class of private, given entities, but rather of the modesty of the claim they make. So what the argument from illusion establishes is not that we always infallibly know what our sense-experience is like, but only that, whether or not we *know* what is the case, we can always say, without much fear of contradiction, what we are inclined to *believe* is the case. These statements do not, then, express a special kind of direct knowledge by acquaintance nor are they premises from which statements about objects could be inferred. For they are not claims to knowledge at all, but more or less tentative expressions of belief, and what is tentatively affirmed is precisely the same as, and thus cannot be a premise for, what, in the conclusion of the supposed inference, we claim to know without hesitation. I shall argue, however, that we can, and rather infrequently do, describe our experience and that we can do this in statements containing such expressions as 'look', 'appear' and 'seem'.

The consequences of this distinction of 'appearances' from sense-data are that knowledge about experience is much less common than is widely supposed and that the greater part of our 'knowledge of appearances' is not capable of figuring as premises in inferences to beliefs about objects.

Before embarking on this another familiar argument for the sense-datum theory must be considered: what may be called the argument from scientific knowledge. There is conclusive evidence for the fact that many of our sense-experiences occur appreciably later than the events of which they give us knowledge, in particular the experiences caused by what is astronomically visible or less remotely audible. More generally, every sense-experience is at the end of a temporally extended causal chain whose first member is the supposedly perceived occurrence. Consequently, what we directly perceive, the object of acquaintance, cannot be the same as that about which we claim knowledge. But this involves no new issue of principle. It shows objects and experiences to be temporally distinct where the argument from illusion shows them to be much more generally different in character. It only shows that we do not directly perceive objects if the supposed consequence of the argument from illusion—that we perceive only our sense-experience directly—is already accepted.

The view common to all versions of the sense-datum theory that the perception of objects is really a kind of inference seems to arise from a belief that, while perception proper must be infallible, inference need not be, and thus that all mistakes are fallacies. But both perception and inference are learnt, intelligent activities which we can presumably perform with varying degrees of efficiency and success. That perception is an acquired skill has perhaps been an inducement to regard it as inference to those who suppose all intelligent activities to be species of reasoning.

Ultimately the problem of perception is that of the relation of thought or language to the world. There is a distressing correspondence with primitive cosmology. Some statements are supported by others, but what supports these others, what is tortoise to their elephant? For the whole system of knowledge cannot support itself in mid-air; it is not self-contained. There is a dilemma here. Either the ultimate support is logically related to the body of knowledge and is thus automatically brought inside the body of knowledge, since only statements can stand in logical relations, and, if so, the question of dependence on the extralinguistic world breaks out again. Or it is not and there is no answer in terms of correct inference to the request for a justification of reliance on this ultimate support.

Philosophers have sought to evade this dilemma by recourse to the Janus-faced notion of experience. The fact that we cannot, it seems, have an experience without somehow being conscious or aware of it has seemed to provide foundation-stones for the edifice of knowledge which are at once statements, capable of standing in logical relations to the rest of the structure, and parts, perhaps the sole constituents, of the extralinguistic world, self-describing entities. I shall contend that there are no such things and opt for the second horn of the dilemma which, as I hope to show, is a less painful resting-place than it might seem.

II

Our first problem is to evaluate the argument from illusion. From the unexceptionable premises that things are not always what they appear to be and that we cannot always tell, there and then, whether they are or not, it is concluded that we have direct knowledge only of appearances, never of objects. For there need be no immediately discoverable difference between two appearances of which one is in fact 'veridical' and the other 'delusive'. So what we really perceive are appearances, whether they are veridical or not depends on something that lies outside the perceptual situation. But what are these appearances that we perceive? They are, it is said, sense-data, the given, immediate experience, they are the current states of our sense-fields.

Of some uses of 'appear', 'seem', etc. it is clearly untrue to say that they figure in descriptions of experience. 'They appear to be away', said when the twice-rung doorbell of a house with drawn curtains remains unanswered, means much the same as 'they must be away' or 'they are probably away'. We are not here describing, but drawing conclusions from, what we observe. The word 'appear' serves to indicate that these conclusions are drawn with less than full confidence. There is nothing 'basic' about them.

But there is another use of 'appear' in which no reason can be given for statements containing it and which do report observations. 'It appears to be green' we might say of a distant house. If challenged we can only repeat, or perhaps correct ourselves or protest, 'well, that is how it appears to me'. But such a statement would normally be made in answer to such questions as 'what colour is that house?' and could be replaced by 'it's green, I think' or 'it's green, isn't it?' They report observations in a tentative way where we know, believe or suspect that the circumstances are unfavourable to an accurate report, that there is something wrong with or abnormal about the conditions of observation. They resemble ordinary categorical descriptions, 'that house is green', in subject-matter, but differ from them in expressing inclinations to believe rather than full beliefs.

There is a third use of 'appear', which resembles the one last mentioned, in that no reasons or evidence can be given for statements containing it, but differs from it in that certain conventional conditions of observation are supposed to obtain, whether they do or not. 'It looks to me (here, now) elliptical' we say of a plate we know to be tilted and round, supposing it to be at right angles to our line of vision. This statement answers the question 'how does it strike you, look to you, what exactly do you see?' It is replaceable by 'there is an elliptical patch in the centre of my visual field'. It is in this type of case only that the description of appearances and experiences coincide.

Consider that old friend the stick half in, half out, of water. One might say of it (a) 'it is straight', (b) 'it looks bent but is really straight', (c) 'it looks bent', (d) 'it is bent'. Statement (a) is true, (b) describes the stick correctly and points out how one might be led to make a mistake about it if unaware of an abnormality (a refracting medium) in the conditions of observation, (c) gives tentative expression to the inclination mistakenly to believe (d) which is straightforwardly false. 'It looks bent' is the puzzling case. For it may be a guarded way of saying 'it is bent' (denied by 'it isn't bent') or a way of saying 'most people would be inclined to say it was bent' (denied by 'it doesn't') or a way of saying 'it looks bent to me, here, now' (which can only be denied by 'oh surely not').

So, even when not used to give tentative conclusions from evidence, the verb 'appear' and its cognates are seldom used to describe experience, but primarily to give tentative descriptions of objects. In other words, the 'appearances' that survive the argument from illusion as the proper objects of acquaintance are not ordinarily sense-experiences. These seemingly rock-bottom matters of fact are, in a way, incorrigible and, *ex hypothesi*, uninferred. But their incorrigibility is imperfect and spurious. Imperfect because both 'this is ϕ, I think' and 'this is ϕ, most people would say' can be contradicted (by 'it isn't and 'they wouldn't') and revised accordingly. Spurious because it arises, not from their making a definite claim about something private, but from their making a weak, indefinite claim about something public. And, though uninferred, they cannot play the part of premises in inferences to categorical descriptions of objects. 'This appears to be ϕ' is no more evidence or a reason for 'this is ϕ' than are 'this may be ϕ' or 'this is probably ϕ'. All three are simply modified ways of saying 'this is ϕ', appropriate for one who is inclined, but not inclined quite confidently enough, to make the categorical statement itself.

This is not to deny that we can and do describe our experience. All I have tried to show is that we describe it very much less often than is usually supposed. Being unsure about the circumstances is a common enough occurrence. But the description of experience proper is a sophisticated procedure and one seldom called for. It is an essential accomplishment for painters, broadcasting engineers, doctors of the eye and ear, cooks and experimental psychologists. But unless we fall into their hands there is little need for us to become proficient in it. The sophistication arises with the deliberate supposition that conditions obtain which we have no reason to suppose do so in fact and perhaps every reason to suppose do not. The fact that we have laboriously to learn perspective drawing is an indication of this, as is the notorious unreliability of eye-witnesses.

That we seldom do describe our experience and then usually with difficulty does not entail that we could not set up and become proficient in the use of a private language. But it would involve a remarkable change in our attitude to the world. Normally we observe in a context of beliefs about where we are and what we are doing that the sophisticated naïveté of phenomenology would exclude. To attend to one's experience involves a radical shift in attitude, a determined effort to resist the solicitations of that submerged constellation of beliefs within which our perceptual discoveries are made.

To this extent, then, I am in sympathy with those who have argued that if the stick half in water looks bent then something really *is* bent. When I say the stick looks bent, I should discover, if I were to direct my attention to it, that my visual field contained a bent brown line. Whether it follows from this that I am in some way aware of this feature of my visual field is a question that will be answered later. But there is something to be said against this line of argument which is commonly ignored. No doubt when the stick looks bent, something else is bent. But consider these cases. I see a small glassy object in a radio shop and say 'that looks like a valve'. But in fact it is a wine-glass. For this error there is no sensory cue; it is the outcome of my general beliefs about the contents of radio shops. Again, I see what is in fact half a pair of spectacles beside a box which I mistakenly suppose to be obscuring the rest. Even when I know better, it still looks just like a pair to me but it is unlikely that my visual field contains anything corresponding to the second lens.

I have been at pains to emphasize the uncommon and sophisticated nature of the description of experience because of the supposed consequence of the argument from illusion, that in every perceptual situation, even if no object is in fact perceived or if objects are misperceived, still something is perceived; our sense-experience. It would seem prima facie that one cannot be said to perceive something unless one is in a position to describe it. But I am not in a position to describe my experience unless I am in the appropriate, sophisticated, phenomenological frame of mind.

Normally if someone says mistakenly that he sees something we are not inclined to say that he really saw something else. We should say of Macbeth that he thought he saw the dagger, imagined he could see it, was under the impression he could see it, but that he did not actually see it at all. In cases of illusion, as against hallucination, there will be something that really is perceived, but it will be a perfectly ordinary public object, not a private experience. If I take a piece of mud on the doormat to be a letter, it will be said that what I actually saw was a piece of mud.

In general, it is not the case, when I am mistaken about what I claim to perceive, either that I am in a position to describe my experience or that I would be said really to have perceived my experience. There are reasons, nevertheless, which have led philosophers to believe that I am aware of my experience, acquainted with it, in such circumstances.

It is not only when in the hands of those professionally concerned with it that we attend to and describe our experience. We are sometimes forced to do so by total ignorance of the conditions of observation. Waking up in unfamiliar circumstances we may, if no other assumption seems inviting, suppose that the conventional phenomen-ological conditions obtain. In exceptional circumstances of this kind, as we come round from an anaesthetic for example, a description of our visual experience is a possible answer to the question 'can you see anything?' But it is worth noticing that in such cases we can also say, with even better warrant perhaps, 'no, just a lot of yellow streaks' instead of 'yes, a lot of yellow streaks'. Only in a very marginal sense is a description of one's visual experience to be called 'seeing' at all.

In a way, then, we can be said sometimes to 'see' our visual experience: when we are trying to describe it or when we are not in a position to describe anything else. But what of the case of a man lying in the sun on his back with his eyes open and his mind far away? Does he see the blue expanse with shifting white patches on it that he could describe if he were to turn his attention to his visual field? And what of the man who is carefully watching a hen to discover where the gap in the hen-run is? Does he see the green expanse of the downs beyond, that he would in fact find occupying the greater part of his visual field if he were to attend to it? Compare these cases with a less problematic kind of seeing. Suppose you show me round your garden and afterwards ask me 'did you see the tulip tree?' If I say 'no', you may say 'you must have done, it's right beside the summer-house I showed you'. If I still deny seeing it, even after another look to refresh my memory, then I cannot have seen it. Yet one might be inclined here to think that I must have seen it all the same. There it was, ten yards away, in broad daylight, right in the middle of my field of vision. But perhaps I was concentrating on the summer-house or thinking of something else altogether. One's visual field is in much the same case as the tulip tree in this example. How-ever far one's attention may have strayed, it seems, nevertheless, that one is inescapably *confronted* by it. So philosophers have said that whenever we think we see anything we really do see the contents of our visual fields. But this is an extremely hypothetical kind of seeing. All we can say is that if I had been in a different frame of mind I should have noticed the tree; I should have been able to describe the contents of my visual field.

In every perceptual situation, then, we know what appears to be the case, but this is not usually to be in a position to describe our experience. It may be true that we can be said to have sense-experiences in every perceptual situation (they are, no doubt, the *causes* of our inclinations to believe) but this is quite another matter from being aware of them, noticing them, being in a position to describe them, and nothing less than this can be involved in the claim of the sense-datum theory that it is our experience which we really perceive.

But can having experiences and being aware of them be clearly distinguished in this way? For having an experience is a mental event of the kind, it would be argued, the only direct evidence for whose existence is its presence in consciousness. One might distinguish two senses of 'awareness'. In the wider sense I am aware of any mental event that I am in any way conscious of. In the narrower sense I am only aware of what I notice or attend to, of what I am in a position to describe, of what, in fact, I have some statable knowledge of. Now it might be argued that one was aware of all experience in the wider sense and that this was sufficient reason for saying that all experience was really perceived. I do not think that this distinction can be maintained. It is not that we are really aware of a great many things which we do not notice or attend to but rather that we suppose ourselves to have a great deal of experience for whose existence we have little or no direct evidence. For ordinarily 'be aware of' and 'notice' are largely interchangeable. Both imply claims to knowledge. There are differences of nuance: to become aware of a smell of decay is to have it borne in upon one, to notice a smell of decay is to have discovered it. In implying claims to knowledge both words resemble the perceptual verbs 'see', 'hear', etc. One cannot be aware *of* something without knowing something about it, being aware *that* something is the case.

Now we are, perhaps, usually vaguely aware of the character of our experience, but far too indefinitely for the knowledge involved to support the complicated structure of beliefs that the sense-datum theory would erect on it. The faint and undetailed nature of this underlying awareness of experience is attested to by the fact that when asked to recall our experience we have more or less to reconstruct it from the objects perceived. We attend to experience often enough to know the sort of experiences normally associated with various kinds of object in various conditions. When we transfer our attention from objects to experience an enormously richer awareness of the latter is obtained. We then suppose that we were in fact having experiences of as complex and detailed a kind while attending to the objects, although we were unaware of the complexity and detail. This move is not inference supported by recollection, but a convention. It is assumed that, given unchanged objects,

medium, and sense-organs, a change of attention brings about no
change in the associated experiences. The idealist's problem 'does
attention alter its object?' is thus a matter of convention not of
fact. The convention described here lays down that it does not. By
this a distinction is introduced between experiences which we have
and which we are aware of. It gives a sense to the expression
'unnoticed experience'. One could equally well, if not better, opt
for the other alternative and speak, not of 'unnoticed', but of
'possible' experiences, that is the experiences one would be aware
of were one to adopt the phenomenological frame of mind. There
is a close analogy with the problem of unsensed sense-data. Should
we speak with Russell of 'sensibilia' or with Ayer of 'possible sense-
data'? In each case considerations of continuity urge one convention,
conceptual economy and epistemological rigour the other. In our
problem continuity makes a stronger claim. For while there is a clear
distinction between sensed and unsensed sense-data, there would
seem to be an unbroken continuum of grades of awareness. At any
rate to have an experience of which one is not aware is not so much
an event as the possibility of an event, it is to be able, by appropriately
directing one's attention, to become aware of an experience. The
nature of these possibilities is discovered inductively. I conclude
that, whether we decide to say we have experiences of which we are
not aware or merely that we could have them, anything we can say
about them or their possibility depends on the limited number we
are aware of. It is only these, meagre or absent in most perceptual
situations, which we can be said to perceive.

III

I have argued that experience cannot be the sole object of acquaintance since it is not the case that in every perceptual situation we are
aware of it. If this argument is accepted it can be reinforced—if not
replaced—by considering what is *meant* by saying that experience alone
is the object of acquaintance. I shall first consider the view that this
is so because only of experience can we have certain knowledge.

That statements about objects can never be certain (an elliptical
way of saying that we can never know for certain that they are true) is
sometimes affirmed on the ground that they are empirical. For it is
an essential feature of empirical statements that they can be shown
to be false and, it is argued, if a statement can be false there can be
reasonable doubt of its truth. But if there can be reasonable doubt

of its truth it cannot be certain. This argument has the notorious consequence that only necessary truths can be certain. This is not, as some have argued, merely inconvenient in assimilating one useful distinction to another, it is the outcome of a definite mistake. For it is not correct to say that a statement is certain only if there *can* be no reasonable doubt of its truth; a statement is certain, rather, if there *is* no reasonable doubt of its truth.

This familiar argument, in trying to prove that no empirical statement is certain, tries to prove too much. For, if it were correct, the supposed difference in epistemological status between objects and experiences could not consist in a difference in respect of certainty between the statements describing them. I shall consider two arguments designed to show that, in fact, there is always reasonable doubt about descriptions of objects. Both assert that descriptions of objects have implications which inevitably 'go beyond' or 'lie outside' the current observation.

The first holds that there is no limit to the set of other statements which follow from a given statement about objects. For at any time, however remote from the time to which the original statement refers, evidence will exist and could be obtained for or against it. If at any time there is no evidence, however tenuous, for or against it, it is then untestable and, therefore, without meaning. At any rate the possibility of evidence arising for any statement, however remote its reference, cannot be ruled out. So, it is argued, however much favourable evidence for the truth of a statement may have accumulated, it is always possible that all the evidence to come may point to and, in the end, enforce the opposite conclusion.

If, as I shall argue later, it is also the case that descriptions of experience can be revised, that there can be evidence for and against them distinct from the occurrence of the experience itself, then precisely the same argument can be applied to them and so no difference in epistemological status is established. In effect this argument comes to the same as the previous one; revision in the face of unfavourable evidence is as much a universal feature of empirical statements as falsifiability.

But, waiving this point for the moment, the argument is fallacious in concluding that statements with 'open consequences' are never certain. For if the statement of unfavourable evidence q is remote, in the way described, from the original statement p, then q alone will not entail the falsity of p but only in conjunction with some generalization or law of nature r. So q will only falsify or disconfirm

p to the extent that r is accepted as true and applicable. It is not p and q simply that are incompatible but p, q and r. If q turns out to be true we are not therefore compelled to abandon p. The more remote q is from p, the more tenuous the connexion, the more we shall be inclined to abandon r. This critical point between abandoning p and abandoning r in face of q may be hard to locate, but for every statement it will exist and for every statement circumstances can be indicated in which its 'logical neighbourhood' is so densely populated with favourable evidence that no remote unfavourable evidence whatever would be taken as refuting it. So it does not follow from the fact that the set of a statement's consequences is open that there is always reasonable doubt of its truth.

The second argument about implications asserts that statements about objects are always and necessarily predictive, that they always logically imply something which the current observation is not sufficient to establish. A statement about objects always forms part of a system of beliefs of varying size, at least including assumptions about the normality—or controllable abnormality—of the conditions of observation. But this has no disastrous consequences. In the first place, no infinite regress is generated. The entailed consequences (or assumptions about the conditions of observation) are themselves statements about objects, but *their* entailed consequences (or conditions) will not all be distinct from the original statement. The implications do not fray off endlessly into the unknown, they are, rather, elements in finite, and indeed decently small, systems of mutual support. And in the second place, arising out of this, it is wrong to regard statements about objects as necessarily predictive under all circumstances. For it is perfectly possible to establish all the members of such a set of mutually supporting statements. Knowledge of the conditions of observation constitutes just such a framework which a statement about objects completes, supports and is supported by. I am not here going back on my earlier criticism of the coherence theory. These coherent sets of statements are not self-sufficient. For their members are conventionally correlated with observed situations. Loose talk about semantic or ostensive rules has ignored the indeterminacy of this correlation, the existence of slack in the application of statements about objects which the systems in which they figure take up.

In the normal course of events it is not that the entailed consequences or conditions are yet to be discovered but that they are known already. This 'systematic' character of our knowledge of objects does indeed distinguish it from our knowledge of experience, consistently with what has gone before since it is the logical correlate of the perceptual as against the phenomenological frame of mind. In the extreme, limiting case (waking up, etc.), where we have no knowledge of the conditions, all descriptions of objects are likely to be less than certain. But we are not usually in this unfortunate position and single observations can give us certain knowledge about objects.

Even if statements about objects were never certain this would not prove them to be derived from statements about experience, if being less than certain were not identified with being probable and if it were not held that nothing can be probable unless something else is certain.

The crucial error in these interconnected doctrines is the supposition that certainty and probability are exhaustive as well as mutually exclusive. Any assertion made with full confidence may be called certain but only one kind of assertion made with less than full confidence is called probable. 'It appears to be cloudy over there' is perfectly good, if weak, evidence for 'it will probably rain'. Yet the whole point of saying that it appears to be, rather than that it is, cloudy over there is to indicate lack of confidence, uncertainty. That is, a less than certain conclusion can be based on less than certain premises which are not themselves the result of inference. The word 'probably' qualifies assertions which are both tentatively advanced, held to be less than certain, and are the conclusions of inferences. This latter characteristic allows us always to challenge, to ask for the reasons for, a statement that something is probably the case and warrants the view that probability is always relative to evidence. But this evidence may itself be tentative and less than certain. To express just this 'uninferred' hesitancy is, as was shown earlier, the principal office of the words 'look', 'appear' and 'seem'. But can we describe experience in this way? The sole use we have for forms of words where these verbs are reiterated (it seems to look ϕ) is where neither verb is used to describe experience (I am inclined to think that most people would say it was ϕ). But this does not entail that phenomenological uses of these verbs cannot be tentative, that 'this looks to me, here, now, ϕ' must be certain. To modify these we use adverbial devices like 'roughly', 'more or less', 'sort of' or add the rider 'I think'. We avoid 'appear' and its kin because they suggest assignable reservations, that we realize or suspect something to be amiss with the conditions of observation or, in non-perceptual uses ('he appears to have died about 300 B.C.'), that we realize that better evidence could, in principle, be obtained. But there are no better conditions in which to describe our experiences than those in which they occur, no better evidence than that they occur. The corrigibility of a statement, in other words, does not entail that 'appear' and the rest apply to it; they apply only where assignable reservations are indicated.

Less than certain statements are not all probable; they are so only if they are the conclusions of inferences, and the premises of these inferences may be less than certain without themselves being inferred. They will be what appears to be the case if I can assign the reservations from which my tentativeness arises or what is, I think, roughly the case, if I cannot.

Finally we must consider a familiar argument against the view that all descriptions of experience are certain. A statement of fact must be expressed by a sentence containing a predicate, a general or descriptive word, and must, therefore, involve the classification of what it refers to, the discrimination of this from other things to which the predicate does not apply. Things, including experiences, do not confront us already sorted out, classified, discriminated. And like any other learnt, regular procedure classification can be carried out wrongly. The use of predicates in classifying and discriminating is essentially a matter of relating what we are describing to the things which are the standard for the application of the predicate, with which it is conventionally correlated, by which it is 'ostensively defined'.

For we can and do revise our descriptions of experience, however convinced we were of their correctness at the time we made them. Such revision could only be excluded by the presumption that re-collected experiences, formerly described as ϕ, and now recalled as noticeably different from something else we want to call ϕ, must always be misrecollected. But our recollections have a credibility of their own which does not depend on what is recollected matching something which we now describe with the same predicate we applied to it. Not only can we revise past descriptions of experience, we can also be hesitant about present descriptions. Sometimes we can find no precedent for a perfectly distinct and definite but unique impression; sometimes, while inclined to give a certain description, there is some peculiarity in the situation which we cannot precisely identify and which makes us hesitate. There is a range of cases between these extremes of inadequate vocabulary and indistinct experience.

Against this view it is argued that the errors corrected by such a revision are merely *verbal*. 'All that one can properly mean... by saying that one doubts whether this (sense-datum) is green is that one is doubting whether "green" is the correct word to use'. (Ayer). But what else is one doubting when one doubts whether this *object* is green? There is a difference, of course, in that one can have another, better, look at the object but not at the sense-datum. But it does not follow from this that all mistakes that do not depend on unfavourable conditions of observation are not really mistakes at all. What, after all, is a 'merely verbal' error? Properly speaking, only mistaken expressions of belief due to slips of the tongue or pen or laziness and inattention. Linguistic incapacity, the source of mistaken descriptions of experience, is quite another matter. Professor Ayer has recently argued that experience is described 'not by relating it to anything else but by indicating that a certain word applies to it in virtue of a meaning rule of the language'. The suggestion is that the application of meaning-rules is such a simple matter that it is impossible to perform it wrongly except by a slip. But meaning-rules do not have the bemusing simplicity of their 'semantic' formulation (the word 'red' applies to red things). The class of things to which a predicate applies is indeterminately bounded. Some blue things are more obviously blue than others. Again we are not equally and perfectly accomplished in the application of all predicates. We can manage 'red' and 'round' fairly well, but are less efficient with 'mauve' and 'rhomboidal'. Even if we were trained up to the highest pitch of descriptive efficiency with the predicates we do understand, it is wrong to imagine that that notoriously blunt instrument, our descriptive vocabulary, would provide a precisely appropriate caption for every situation, that it could deal exhaustively with the fecundity of experience. Behind this theory of semantic rules lurks a pair of metaphysical assumptions: that universals, in one-one correlation with predicates, are wide open to some kind of direct apprehension and that there is a decent limit to their variety. The implied analogy with the rules by means of which the truths of mathematics and logic are established is misleading. These rules are precise, definite and can be clearly stated and communicated; careful tests can be made of whether they have been employed correctly. No such laborious check of the correct employment of 'meaning-rules' is possible with the private, fluid and unstable constituents of our sense-experience.

Lack of clarity about the relation between the mere occurrence of an experience and its description has contributed to the view that we cannot, without lying or slips, misdescribe experience. Experience just happens. But being what it is we cannot help being aware of it. Yet it occurs in every perceptual situation. This confusion of the phenomenologically scrutinized with the more or less hypothetical unnoticed experience is responsible for the view that simply to have an experience is to know it for what it is. Those who have, consistently enough, denied that experience as such is properly speaking either a kind of knowledge or true or false at all, have avoided the confusion at the cost of abolishing their problem. For from mere events nothing can be logically derived; only from statements, from what can be known to be true, can other statements be inferred.

I conclude that statements about objects and about experience are sometimes certain, sometimes not. In this respect there is no sharp distinction between the two. Whether a description of objects is certain will depend largely on the circumstances in which it is given and what is known about them. Its familiarity and stability will no doubt determine whether a description of experience is certain. We can err about both from linguistic incapacity and the loose correlation of language and the world, about objects on account of unfavourable conditions of observation and about experiences (and occasionally objects) on account of their evanescence. Such difference as there is between the respective sources of error is not sufficient to substantiate a theory of acquaintance or to show one category to be logically prior to the other.

IV

Some philosophers, realising that certainty as a criterion of acquaintance or basic statements is not sufficient to distinguish objects and experience in the way the sense-datum theory requires, have proposed a different definition in terms of inference. On this view we know directly, by acquaintance, what we know without inference; basic statements are primitive, uninferred; and, while no descriptions of experience are inferred, all descriptions of objects are. The task of theory of knowledge, it is held, is to make a rational reconstruction of our knowledge of matters of fact in which the uninferred premises from which alone this knowledge can be validly derived are explicitly set out. It is agreed that we are rarely, if ever, conscious of carrying out these inferences. It is thought, nevertheless, that experiential premises must somehow 'underlie' what we believe about objects.

If this account is correct two conditions must be satisfied. Statements about experience must count as reasons or evidence for statements about objects and they must in some, no doubt rather obscure, sense be accepted by those who make statements about objects. This second, seemingly platitudinous, requirement deserves emphasis. A fact cannot be a man's reason or evidence for an assertion unless, however implicitly, he is aware of it. Someone's implicit or unconscious awareness of facts about objects can be established by observation of his behaviour. But there is no such criterion available for detecting his awareness of his experience. The view, mistaken as I have argued, that we cannot help being aware of our experience no doubt explains why it has not been thought necessary to provide any criterion for the occurrence of this supposed awareness. If my argument against the view that in every perceptual situation we are aware of our own experience is accepted, it follows that the second condition of the inference theory is unsatisfied and that the theory is mistaken. For our experiences could only be our reasons or evidence for our beliefs about objects if we were to become aware of them through adopting a completely different, phenomenological, frame of mind in our traffic with the external world. Like any other facts, facts about experience must be discovered before they can be appealed to. But even if my argument on this is not accepted, the inference theory is mistaken since the first condition mentioned is not satisfied either.

The best proof that statements about experience were reasons or evidence for statements about objects would be that we did in fact commonly infer from the one to the other. This, however, is admittedly not the case. But, as it stands, this is of little importance. In the first place, the psychological criterion involved is exceedingly vague, seeming to do no more than mark off as cases of inference those in which a thoughtful pause supervenes between observation and announcement. Furthermore, there are many cases, unquestionably of knowledge by inference, where it is not in the least likely that any conscious process of reasoning has taken place. A girl, sitting in the drawing-room, hears the front door slam and says 'Father's home'. I hear a pattering on the roof and say 'it's raining'. I see a small pool on the kitchen floor and say 'the dog has misbehaved'. We only infer consciously in situations that are unfamiliar or complex, in the predicament of the weekend guest or the new boy on the first day of term. The detective, the busybody, the scientist are more or less professionally concerned to make the most of a small stock of data. Conscious, deliberate thinking is both exhausting and infrequent, a last resort to be appealed to only when all habitual capacities have failed. But most of our perceptual knowledge is of familiar states of affairs and acquired in familiar conditions.

That a statement is employed as a premise in a conscious process of reasoning is not the only feature of our use of that statement which shows it to count as a reason or evidence for the conclusion. More fundamental surely, is that we *give* it as our reason when challenged on the other.

Consider these five cases. I can at once reproduce the course of reasoning that led me to say that it is Mother's hat on top of the garage. This is conscious inference, where the reason given is a premise already consciously affirmed. Secondly, I can, without hesitation, answer 'by the way he sways about' when asked how I can tell someone is drunk, although I recollect no process of inferring. Thirdly, I may take some time over or require assistance in accounting for my claim that Towzer is ill by the glazed look in his eye. Fourthly, I may be unable to give any reason of my own and unwilling to accept any reason offered by another for my assertion that X dislikes Y. Yet commonly in this type of case I may be sure a reason does exist for my belief, may be extremely confident of the truth of my belief and turn out, in the end, to be quite right. Finally, consider standing in broad daylight three feet away from a large and perfectly normal chestnut cart-horse and saying 'that is a horse' or, more adventurously, 'that horse is brown'. This resembles the previous case in that one would be quite unable to give or accept any reason whatever for one's assertion. It differs from it in that one would not be in the very least abashed or apologetic about this. For, in these conditions, the challenge 'how can you tell?' is simply devoid of sense.

Still, if it were made, one might perhaps answer 'well, because it looks like a horse'. If this were intended as a description of one's experience, as interchangeable with 'there is now a shiny brown patch of a characteristic shape in the centre of my visual field', it would not be to answer the question but rather to change the subject, perhaps to offer a causal explanation of one's belief. But this interpretation proposed by the sense-datum theory, a wildly unnatural interpretation of what is, in the circumstances, a wildly unnatural remark, is surely mistaken. The statement would more naturally be intended and understood as a modification of, an infusion of tentativeness into, the original claim, expressing a lack of confidence inspired by the nagging question. As such it is not a reason. To repeat oneself in a more cautious way is not to substantiate but merely to attenuate one's original assertion. 'It looks like a horse' resembles 'it is probably a horse' or 'I think it's a horse' and not 'it has thick legs and no horns' which might be advanced to support the claim that some comparatively distant animal was a horse. For there are, of course, plenty of situations in which reasons do exist for statements about objects.

A statement cannot be inferred, then, if no reason or evidence for it exists, or, more exactly, if it does not make sense to ask for or give a reason for it. Whether or not it does make sense to ask for a reason depends on the circumstances in which the statement is made. The sentence, the form of words, 'that is a horse', may be used in an enormous variety of circumstances. In some of these it will make sense to ask 'how can you tell', in others not. The latter may be called the standard conditions of its use. It will be in such circumstances that the use of the sentence will normally be learnt. This accomplished, it will be possible to use it in an increasingly adventurous way in increasingly non-standard conditions. Connexions are established between assertions and their reasons through the discovery of a vast array of factual concomitances. That standard conditions are those in which we learn how to use a sentence helps to explain why the statements they are used to make are basic and uninferred. For in these conditions they are directly correlated with an observable situation, they are not introduced by means of other statements. (This explains 'implicit inference'. I implicitly infer, acknowledge a reason for, a statement if I was introduced to it by means of other statements but can now make it without conscious consideration of them.) For some sentences there are no standard conditions (generalizations or such implicitly general sentences as 'she is naturally shy'). With others the nature of their standard conditions may vary from person to person. A wife will be able to tell at once that her husband is depressed where others have no inkling of the fact. (A difference in capacity that leads us to speak of intuition.) Again prolonged success in a certain nonstandard use of a sentence may lead us to incorporate the conditions of this use into the standard. I say 'it is raining' when I cannot actually see the rain falling but only drops of water bouncing off the wet street. The addition of unwillingness or inability to answer the question 'how can you tell?' shows that these conditions have become standard. Standard conditions are those in which we have a right to feel certain of the truth of an assertion. The suggestion of uncertainty conveyed by the protest 'that's only an inference' would be made more obviously by the equivalent protest 'you are in no position to be sure' (i.e., 'these are not standard conditions'.) The lawyer, who asks for a description of what one *actually* saw, devoid of inference and conjecture, is asking for a standard description, that is, a description for which the conditions one was then in were standard.

The notions of acquaintance and of the basic statements which it warrants have, therefore, a foundation in our ordinary way of thinking and speaking. The failure to locate them in their right place is due in part to the failure to distinguish between sentences and statements. For because of multiplicity of uses there are no 'basic sentences'. What we know for certain and without inference in any situation is what the circumstances we are in are the standard conditions for. This will normally be a statement about objects. But there are circumstances in which, knowing nothing about the conditions or that they are highly abnormal, we can take no description of objects as standard. In such a situation we can do no more than tentatively say what appears to be the case. If we are not prepared to do this we can, by an appropriate shift of attention, describe our experience. This last-ditch feature of statements about experience is another encouragement to the sense-datum theorist.

More important is the fact that standard conditions are not a perfect guarantee of the truth of a statement made in them. For standard conditions do not involve that all of a statement's entailed consequences have been established. The horse in the example may just possibly be a brilliantly contrived deception, a flat painted board. We could make our standard stringent enough to cater for this, by insisting on the establishment of entailed consequences, without abandoning statements about objects as basic. But it would be laborious and inconvenient to do so. The programme of convenience embodied in our actual standards is abetted by the order of nature which is uniform enough to make the risks of standard description negligible. Our standards depend on contingencies but some contingencies are highly reliable and regular. Error, as Descartes pointed out, is a product of the will rather than the understanding and arises almost entirely with nonstandard descriptions.

This minute residual imperfection is the ultimate source of the sense-datum theory. The metaphysical demand behind the theory is for an infallible basis for knowledge. So a new standard is proposed which is thought to be perfect. The justification of the new standard is that the knowledge of conditions required is always available, conditions are always standard for the description of experience. I have argued that we are not, in fact, always in standard conditions for the description of experience but rather that it is always in our power, by an appropriate shift of attention, to produce such conditions. If this is so, the sense-datum theory can be no more than the proposal of a new and exceedingly cumbrous way of thinking and speaking to be adopted from fear of a very minor risk. But whether it is true or not, whether the sense-datum theory is a proposal or, what it claims to be, an account of what actually occurs, the supposed improvement is illusory. For, in taking steps to set one exaggerated doubt at rest, it provides the opportunity for another to arise. Admittedly descriptions of experience, for which conditions are always standard, do not depend on a knowledge of conditions which may not be forthcoming. But they have weaknesses of their own. The objects we describe are largely stable and persistent; if we are unsure about them we can always look again. But experience is fleeting and momentary; to attend to it again is to make the insecure hypothesis that it has not changed. The systematic, mutually corroborative character of our beliefs about objects is not a weakness but a strength. Similarly the atomic, disconnected character of experiences, which has encouraged the view that they are self-describing entities, is a weakness. I conclude, then, that experiences are not only not in fact the basis of our empirical knowledge but that they would be inferior to the basis we have, since we are just as much open to error about them, though not in entirely the same way; and we should have to revise our way of thinking and speaking completely to use them as a basis.

The relation between experiences and objects, then, neither is nor should be logical. On the contrary it is causal, a matter of psychological fact. Our beliefs about objects are based on experience in a way that requires not justification but explanation. Experiences are not *my* reasons for my beliefs about objects—to have an experience is not to know or believe anything which could be a reason in this sense—though they may be the reasons for my believing what I do from the point of view of the psychologist. They may, that is, be the causes of my beliefs and explain them. But they could only be my reasons for my beliefs about objects if I already knew something independently about the relations between experiences and objects.

We learn, it is said, to interpret our experiences, to give rein to Hume's principle of the imagination, to apply Kant's schematized category of substance. These forms of words at least point out that perception is an intelligent activity (not an infallible reflex), but they point it out so uncompromisingly that it is overintellectualised. Interpreting experiences suggests literary scholarship or detective work. But not all intellectual processes are types of reasoning. These phrases refer to the psychological preconditions of recognizing objects for what they are. They point out that we must learn to use the language we do use, that this is an exercise of skill not an automatism and, further, that the situations in which any one sentence may be correctly uttered are extremely various. But they do not demand and could not evoke any logical justification of our practice of thinking and speaking of a common world of objects. We cannot set out the logical relation of an assertion about objects with the experiences that occasion it, because there is no such relation. This is not to sever language from the world altogether, the sin of the coherence theory. It is simply to say that the relations that obtain within the body of our knowledge do not also connect it with what is outside.

I have considered the three principal methods of establishing the sense-datum theory: the arguments from illusion, certainty and inference. Those who hold statements about experience to be basic have misconstrued all three. Statements about experience are not known in every perceptual situation, for we cannot know what we are not aware of, they are no more certain than statements about objects and they do not differ from all statements about objects in being uninferred. Doctrines about acquaintance and basic statements are the outcome of a search for perfect standard conditions. But no standard conditions are perfect and there is no reason to say that descriptions of experience are or ought to be our standard. Our empirical knowledge already has a basis and as good a one as we can obtain. It is to be found, as we should expect, in those situations in which the use of our language is taught and learnt.

IV

THE CAUSAL THEORY OF PERCEPTION

1. H. P. GRICE

I

THE Causal Theory of Perception (CTP) has for some time received comparatively little attention, mainly, I suspect, because it has been generally assumed that the theory either asserts or involves as a consequence the proposition that material objects are unobservable, and that the unacceptability of this proposition is sufficient to dispose of the theory. I am inclined to regard this attitude to the CTP as unfair or at least unduly unsympathetic and I shall attempt to outline a thesis which might not improperly be considered to be a version of the CTP, and which is, if not true, at least not too obviously false.

What is to count as holding a causal theory of perception? (1) I shall take it as being insufficient merely to believe that the perception of a material object is always to be causally explained by reference to conditions the specification of at least one of which involves a mention of the object perceived; that, for example, the perception is the terminus of a causal sequence involving at an earlier stage some event or process in the history of the perceived object. Such a belief does not seem to be philosophical in character; its object has the appearance of being a very general contingent proposition; though it is worth remarking that if the version of the CTP with which I shall be primarily concerned is correct, it (or something like it) will turn out to be a necessary rather than a contingent truth. (2) It may be held that the elucidation of the notion of perceiving a material object will include some reference to the rôle of the material object perceived in the causal ancestry of the perception or of the sense-impression or sense-datum involved in the perception). This contention is central to what I regard as a standard version of the CTP. (3) It might be held that it is the task of the philosopher of perception not to elucidate or character-

Symposium by H. P. Grice and Alan R. White. From *Proceedings of the Aristotelian Society*, Supp. Vol. 35 (1961), pp. 121–68. Reprinted by courtesy of the authors and the Editor of the Aristotelian Society.

ize the ordinary notion of perceiving a material object, but to provide a rational reconstruction of it, to replace it by some concept more appropriate to an ideal or scientific language: it might further be suggested that such a redefinition might be formulated in terms of the effect of the presence of an object upon the observer's sense-organ and nervous system or upon his behaviour or 'behaviour-tendencies' or in terms of both of these effects. A view of this kind may perhaps deserve to be called a causal theory of perception; but I shall not be concerned with theories on these lines. (4) I shall distinguish from the adoption of a CTP the attempt to provide for a wider or narrower range of propositions ascribing properties to material objects a certain sort of causal analysis: the kind of analysis which I have in mind is that which, on *one* possible interpretation, Locke could be taken as suggesting for ascriptions of, for example, colour and temperature; he might be understood to be holding that such propositions assert that an object would, in certain standard conditions, cause an observer to have certain sorts of ideas or sense-impressions.

In Professor Price's *Perception*,[1] there appears a preliminary formulation of the CTP which would bring it under the second of the headings distinguished in the previous paragraph. The CTP is specified as maintaining (1) that in the case of all sense-data (not merely visual and tactual 'belonging to' simply means *being caused by*, so that '*M* is present to my senses' will be equivalent to '*M* causes a sense-datum with which I am acquainted'; (2) that perceptual consciousness is fundamentally an inference from effect to cause. Since it is, I think, fair to say[2] that the expression 'present to my senses' was introduced by Price as a special term to distinguish one of the possible senses of the verb 'perceive', the first clause of the quotation above may be taken as propounding the thesis that 'I am perceiving *M*' (in one sense of that expression) is to be regarded as equivalent to 'I am having (or sensing) a sense-datum which is caused by *M*'. (The second clause I shall for the time being ignore.) I shall proceed to consider at some length the feature which this version of the CTP shares with other non-causal theories of perception, namely, the claim that perceiving a material object involves having or sensing a sense-datum; for unless this claim can be made out the special features of the CTP become otiose.

[1] p. 66.
[2] Cf. ibid., pp. 21–25.

II

The primary difficulty facing the contention that perceiving involves having or sensing a sense-datum is that of giving a satisfactory explanation of the meaning of the technical term 'sense-datum'. One familiar method of attempting this task is that of trying to prove, by means of some form of the Argument from Illusion, the existence of objects of a special sort for which the term 'sense-datum' is offered as a class-name. Another method (that adapted in a famous passage by Moore) is that of giving directions which are designed to enable one to pick out items of the kind to which the term 'sense-datum' is to be applied. The general character of the objections to each of these procedures is also familiar, and I shall, for present purposes, assume that neither procedure is satisfactory.

Various philosophers have suggested that though attempts to indicate, or demonstrate the existence of, special objects to be called sense-data have all failed, nevertheless the expression 'sense-datum' can (and should) be introduced as a technical term; its use would be explicitly defined by reference to such supposedly standard locutions as 'So-and-so looks ϕ (e.g., blue) to me', 'It looks (feels) to me as if there were a ϕ so-and-so', 'I seem to see something ϕ' and so on. Now as the objection to such proposals which I have in mind is one which might be described as an objection in principle, it is not to my present purpose to consider how in detail such an explicit definition of the notion of a sense-datum might be formulated. I should, however, remark that this programme may be by no means so easy to carry through as the casual way in which it is sometimes proposed might suggest; various expressions are candidates for the key role in this enterprise e.g., 'looks' ('feels' etc.), 'seems', 'appears' and the more or less subtle differences between them would have to be investigated; and furthermore even if one has decided on a preferred candidate, not all of its uses would be suitable; if for example we decide to employ the expressions 'looks' etc., are we to accept the legitimacy of the sentence 'It looks indigestible to me' as providing us with a sense-datum sentence 'I am having an indigestible visual sense-datum'?

A general objection to the suggested procedure might run as follows: When someone makes such a remark as 'It looks red to me' a certain implication is carried, an implication which is disjunctive in form. It is implied either that the object referred to is known or believed by the speaker not to *be* red, *or* that it has been denied by someone else to be red, *or* that the speaker is doubtful whether it is red, *or* that someone else has expressed doubt whether it is red, *or* that the situation is such that though no doubt has actually been expressed and no denial has actually been made, some person or other might feel inclined towards denial or doubt if he were to address himself to the question whether the object is actually red. This may not be an absolutely exact or complete characterization of the implication, but it is perhaps good enough to be going on with. Let us refer to the condition which is fulfilled when one or other of the limbs of this disjunction is true as the *D*-or-*D* condition ('doubt or denial' condition). Now we may perhaps agree that there is liable to be something odd or even absurd about employing an 'It looks to me' locution when the appropriate *D*-or-*D* condition is fairly obviously not fulfilled; there would be something at least prima facie odd about my saying 'That looks red to me' (not as a joke) when I am confronted by a British pillar box in normal daylight at a range of a few feet. At this point my objector advances a twofold thesis, (*a*) that it is a feature of the use, perhaps of the meaning, of such locutions as 'looks to me' that they should carry the implication that the *D*-or-*D* condition is fulfilled, and that if they were uttered by a speaker who did not suppose this condition was fulfilled he would be guilty of a misuse of the locutions in question (unless of course he were intending to deceive his audience into thinking that the condition was fulfilled), (*b*) that in cases where the *D*-or-*D* condition is unfulfilled the utterance employing the 'looks to me' locution, so far from being uninterestingly true, is neither true nor false. Thus armed, my objector now assails the latter-day sense-datum theorist. Our every day life is populated with cases in which the sensible characteristics of the things we encounter are not the subject of any kind of doubt or controversy; consequently there will be countless situations in which the employment of 'looks to me' idioms would be out of order and neither true nor false. But the sense-datum theorist wants his sense-datum statements to be such that some one or more of them is true whenever a perceptual statement is true; for he wants to go on to give a *general* analysis of perceptual statements in terms of the notion of sense-data. But this goal must be unattainable if 'looks to me' statements (and so sense-datum statements) can be truly made only in the *less* straightforward perceptual situations; and if the goal is unattainable the CTP collapses.

It is of course possible to take a different view of the linguistic phenomena outlined in my previous paragraph. One may contend that if I were to say 'it looks red to me' in a situation in which the *D*-or-*D* condition is not fulfilled, what I say is (subject to certain qualifications) true, not 'neuter'; while admitting that though true it might be very misleading and that its truth might be very boring and its misleadingness very important, one might still hold that its *suggestio falsi* is perfectly compatible with its literal truth. Furthermore one might argue that though perhaps someone who, without intent to deceive, employed the 'it looks to me' locution when he did not suppose the D-or-D condition to be fulfilled would be guilty in some sense of a misuse of *language*, he could be said not to be guilty of a misuse of the particular locution in question; for, one might say, the implication of the fulfilment of the D-or-D condition attaches to such locutions not as a special feature of the meaning or use of these expressions, but in virtue of a general feature or principle of the use of language. The mistake of supposing the implication to constitute a 'part of the meaning' of 'looks to me' is somewhat similar to, though more insidious than, the mistake which would be made if one supposed that the so-called implication that one believes it to be raining was 'a part of the meaning' of the expression 'it is raining'. The short and literally inaccurate reply to such a supposition might be that the so-called implication attaches because the expression is a propositional one, not because it is the particular propositional expression which it happens to be.

Until fairly recently it seemed to me to be very difficult indeed to find any arguments which seemed at all likely to settle the issue between these two positions. One might, for example, suggest that it is open to the champion of sense-data to lay down that the sense-datum sentence 'I have a pink sense-datum' should express a truth if and only if the facts are as they would have to be for it to be true, *if it were in order*, to say 'Something looks pink to me', even though it may not actually be in order to say this (because the D-or-D condition is unfulfilled). But this attempt to by-pass the objector's position would be met by the reply that it begs the question; for it assumes that there is some way of specifying the facts in isolation from the implication standardly carried by such a specification; and this is precisely what the objector is denying. As a result of frustrations of this kind, I was led to suspect that neither position should be regarded as right or wrong, but that the linguistic phenomena *could* be looked at in either way, though there might be reasons for preferring to adopt one way of viewing them rather than the other; that there might be no proofs or disproofs, but only inducements. On this assumption I was inclined to rule against my objector, partly because his opponent's position was more in line with the kind of thing I was inclined to say about other linguistic phenomena which are in some degree comparable, but mainly because the objector's short way with sense-data is an even shorter way with scepticism about the material world; and I think a sceptic might complain that though his worries may well prove dissoluble he ought at least to be able to state them; if we do not allow him to state them we cannot remove the real source of his discomfort. However, I am now inclined to think that the issue is a decidable one, and that my objector's position is wrong and that of his opponent right. I shall attempt to develop a single argument (though no doubt there are others) to support this claim, and as a preliminary I shall embark on a discursus about certain aspects of the concept or concepts of implication, using some more or less well-worn examples.

III

(*Implication*)

I shall introduce four different examples and use upon them four different ideas as catalysts. All are cases in which in ordinary parlance, or at least in philosophical parlance, something might be said to be implied as distinct from being stated.

(1)'Smith has left off beating his wife', where what is implied is that Smith has been beating his wife.

(2)'She was poor but she was honest', where what is implied is (very roughly) that there is some contrast between poverty and honesty, or between her poverty and her honesty.

The first example is a stock case of what is sometimes called 'presupposition' and it is often held that here the truth of what is implied is a necessary condition of the original statement's being either true or false. This might be disputed, but it is at least arguable that it is so, and its being arguable might be enough to distinguish this type of case from others. I shall however for convenience assume that the common view mentioned is correct. This consideration clearly distinguishes (1) from (2); even if the implied proposition were false, i.e. if there were no reason in the world to contrast poverty with honesty either in general or in her case, the original statement could still be false; it would be false if for example she were rich and dishonest. One might perhaps be less comfortable about assenting to its truth if the implied contrast did not in fact obtain; but the possibility of falsity is enough for the immediate purpose.

My next experiment on these examples is to ask what it is in each case which could properly be said to be the vehicle of implication (to do the implying). There are at least four candidates, not necessarily mutually exclusive. Supposing someone to have uttered one or other of my sample sentences, we may ask whether the vehicle of implication would be (a) what the speaker said (or asserted), or (b) the speaker ('did he imply that . . . . ') or (c) the words the speaker used, or (d) his saying that (or again his saying that in that way); or possibly some plurality of these items. As regards (a) I think (1) and (2) differ; I think it would be correct to say in the case of (1) that what the speaker said (or asserted) implied that Smith had been beating his wife, and incorrect to say in the case of (2) that what he said (or asserted) implied that there was a contrast between e.g., honesty and poverty. A test on which I would rely is the following: if accepting that the implication holds involves one in accepting an hypothetical 'if p then q' where 'p' represents the original statement and 'q' represents what is implied, then what the speaker said (or asserted) is a vehicle of implication, otherwise not. To apply this rule to the given examples, if I accepted the implication alleged to hold in the case of (1), I should feel compelled to accept the hypothetical 'If Smith has left off beating his wife, then he has been beating her'; whereas if I accepted the alleged implication in the case of (2), I should not feel compelled to accept the hypothetical 'If she was poor but honest, then there is some contrast between poverty and honesty, or between her poverty and her honesty'. The other candidates can be dealt with more cursorily; I should be inclined to say with regard to both (1) and (2) that the speaker could be said to have implied whatever it is that is implied; that in the case of (2) it seems fairly clear that the speaker's words could be said to imply a contrast, whereas it is much less clear whether in the case of (1) the speaker's words could be said to imply that Smith had been beating his wife; and that in neither case would it be evidently appropriate to speak of his saying that, or of his saying that in that way, as implying what is implied.

The third idea with which I wish to assail my two examples is really a twin idea, that of the detachability or cancellability of the implication. (These terms will be explained.) Consider example (1): one cannot find a form of words which could be used to state or assert *just* what the sentence 'Smith has left off beating his wife' might be used to assert such that when it is used the implication that Smith has been beating his wife is just absent. *Any* way of asserting what is asserted in (1) involves the implication in question. I shall express this fact by saying that in the case of (1) the implication is not *detachable* from what is asserted (or *simpliciter*, is not detachable). Furthermore, one cannot take a form of words for which both what is asserted and what is implied is the same as for (1), and *then* add a further clause withholding commitment from what would otherwise be implied, with the idea of annulling the implication without annulling the assertion. One cannot intelligibly say 'Smith has left off beating his wife but I do not mean to imply that he has been beating her'. I shall express this fact by saying that in the case of (1) the implication is not *cancellable* (without cancelling the assertion). If we turn to (2) we find, I think, that there is quite a strong case for saying that here the implication *is* detachable. There seems quite a good case for maintaining that if, instead of saying 'She is poor but she is honest' I were to say 'She is poor and she is honest', I would assert just what I would have asserted if I had used the original sentence; but there would now be no implication of a contrast between e.g., poverty and honesty. But the question whether, in the case of (2), the implication is cancellable, is slightly more complex. There is a sense in which we may say that it is non-cancellable; if someone were to say 'She is poor but she is honest, though of course I do not mean to imply that there is any contrast between poverty and honesty', this would seem a puzzling and eccentric thing to have said; but though we should wish to quarrel with the speaker, I do not think we should go so far as to say that his utterance was *unintelligible*; we should suppose that he had adopted a most peculiar way of conveying the news that she was poor *and* honest.

The fourth and last test that I wish to impose on my examples is to ask whether we would be inclined to regard the fact that the appropriate implication is present as being a matter of the meaning of some particular word or phrase occurring in the sentences in question. I am aware that this may not be always a very clear or easy question to answer; nevertheless I will risk the assertion that we would be fairly happy to say that, as regards (2), the fact that the implication obtains is a matter of the meaning of the word 'but'; whereas so far as (1) is concerned we should have at least some inclination to say that the presence of the implication was a matter of the meaning of some of the words in the sentence, but we should be in some difficulty when it came to specifying precisely which this word is, or words are, of which this is true.

I may now deal more briefly with my remaining examples.

(3) I am reporting on a pupil at Collections. All I say is 'Jones has

beautiful handwriting and his English is grammatical'. We might perhaps agree that there would here be a strong, even overwhelming, implication that Jones is no good at philosophy. It is plain that there is no case at all for regarding the truth of what is implied here as a pre-condition of the truth or falsity of what I have asserted; a denial of the truth of what is implied would have no bearing at all on whether what I have asserted is true or false. So (3) is much closer to (2) than (1) in this respect. Next, I (the speaker) could certainly be said to have implied that Jones is hopeless (provided that this is what I intended to get across) and my saying that (at any rate my saying *just* that and no more) is also certainly a vehicle of implication. On the other hand my words and what I say (assert) are, I think, not here vehicles of implication. (3) thus differs from both (1) and (2). The implication is cancellable but not detachable; if I add 'I do not of course mean to imply that he is no good at philosophy' my whole utterance is intelligible and linguistically impeccable, even though it may be extraordinary tutorial behaviour; and I can no longer be said to have implied that he was no good, even though perhaps that is what my colleagues might conclude to be the case if I had nothing else to say. The implication is not, however, detachable; any other way of making, in the same context of utterance, *just* the assertion I have made would involve the same implication. Finally, the fact that the implication holds is not a matter of any particular word or phrase within the sentence which I have uttered; so in this respect (3) is certainly different from (2) and possibly different from (1).

One obvious fact should be mentioned before I pass to the last example. This case of implication is unlike the others in that the utterance of the sentence 'Jones has beautiful handwriting etc.' does not *standardly* involve the implication here attributed to it; it requires a special context (that it should be uttered at Collections) to *attach* the implication to its utterance.

(4) If someone says 'My wife is either in the kitchen or in the bedroom' it would normally be implied that he did not know in *which* of the two rooms she was.

This example might well be held to be very similar to the case under dispute, that of such statements as 'This looks red to me' so I must be careful not to prejudge any issues to my objector's disadvantage.

I think, however, that in the case of (4) I can produce a strong argument in favour of holding that the fulfilment of the implication of the speaker's ignorance is not a pre-condition of the truth or falsity of the disjunctive statement. Suppose (*a*) that the speaker knows that his wife is in the kitchen, (*b*) that the house has only two rooms (and no passages etc.) Even though (*a*) is the case, the speaker can certainly say truly 'My wife is in the house'; he is merely not being as informative as he could be if need arose. But the true proposition that his wife is in the house together with the true proposition that the house consists entirely of a kitchen and a bedroom, entail the proposition that his wife is either in the kitchen or in the bedroom. But if to express the proposition *p* in certain circumstances would be to speak truly, and *p*, together with another true proposition, entails *q*, then surely to express *q* in the *same* circumstances must be to speak truly. So I shall take it that the disjunctive statement in (4) does not fail to be true or false if the implied ignorance is in fact not realized. Secondly, I think it is fairly clear that in this case, as in the case of (3), we could say that the *speaker* had implied that he did not know, and also that *his saying that* (or his saying that rather than something else, viz., in which room she was) implied that he did not know. Thirdly, the implication is in a sense non-detachable, in that if *in a given context* the utterance of the disjunctive sentence would involve the implication that the speaker did not know in which room his wife was, this implication would also be involved in the utterance of any other form of words which would make the same assertion (e.g., 'The alternatives are (1) .... (2) .... ' or 'One of the following things is the case: (*a*) .... (*b*) .... '). In *another* possible sense, however, the implication could perhaps be said to be detachable; for there will be *some* contexts of utterance in which the normal implication will not hold; e.g., the spokesman who announces, 'The next conference will be either in Geneva or in New York' perhaps does not imply that he does not know which; for he may well be just not saying which. This points to the fact that the implication is cancellable; a man could say, 'My wife is either in the kitchen or in the bedroom' in circumstances in which the implication would normally be present, and then go on, 'Mind you, I'm not saying that I don't know which'; this might be unfriendly (and perhaps ungrammatical) but would be perfectly intelligible. Finally, the fact that the utterance of the disjunctive sentence normally involves the implication of the speaker's ignorance of the truth-values of the disjuncts is, I should like to say, to be explained by reference to a general principle governing the use of language. Exactly what this principle is I am uncertain, but a *first shot* would be the following: 'One should not make a weaker statement rather than a stronger one unless there is a good reason for so doing.' This is certainly not an adequate formulation but will perhaps be good enough for my present purpose. On the assumption that such a principle as this is of general application, one can draw the conclusion that the utterance of a disjunctive sentence would imply the speaker's ignorance of the truth-values of the disjuncts, given that (a) the obvious reason for not making a statement which there is some call on one to make is that one is not in a position to make it, and given (b) the logical fact that each disjunct entails the disjunctive, but not *vice versa*; which being so, the disjuncts are stronger than the disjunctive. If the outline just given is on the right lines, then I would wish to say, we have a reason for refusing in the case of (4) to regard the implication of the speaker's ignorance as being part of the meaning of the word 'or'; someone who knows about the logical relation between a disjunction and its disjuncts, and who also knew about the alleged general principle governing discourse, could work out for himself that disjunctive utterances would involve the implication which they do in fact involve. I must insist, however, that my aim in discussing this last point has been merely to indicate the position I would wish to take up, and not to argue seriously in favour of it.

My main purpose in this sub-section has been to introduce four ideas of which I intend to make some use; and to provide some conception of the ways in which they apply or fail to apply to various types of implication. I do not claim to have presented a systematic theory of implication; that would be a very large undertaking and one for another occasion.

IV

(The objection reconsidered)

Let us now revert to the main topic of this section of my paper. Let us call a statement of the type expressible by such a sentence as 'it looks red to me' an *L*-statement. What are we to say of the relation between an *L*-statement and the corresponding *D*-or-*D* condition, in terms of the ideas introduced in the previous sub-section? Or, rather, since this might be controversial, what would my objector think it correct to say on this subject? As I have represented his position, he is explicitly committed to holding that the fulfilment of the appropriate *D*-or-*D* condition is a necessary pre-condition of an *L*-statement's being either true or false. He is also more or less explicitly committed to holding that the implication that the *D*-or-*D* condition is fulfilled is a matter of the meaning of the word 'looks' (or of the phrase 'looks to me'); that, for example, someone who failed to realise that there existed this implication would *thereby* show that he did not fully understand the meaning of the expression or phrase in question. It is conceivable that this last-mentioned thesis is independent of the rest of his position, that he could if necessary abandon it without destroying the remainder of his position. I shall not, therefore, in what follows address myself directly to this point, though I have hopes that it may turn out to be *solutum ambulando*. Next, he would, I think, wish to say that the implication of the fulfilment of the D-or-D condition is neither detachable nor cancellable; but even if he should not wish to say this, he certainly *must* say it if his objection is to be of any importance. For if the implication is detachable or cancellable, all that the sense-datum theorist needs to do is to find some form of words from which the implication is detached or in which it is cancelled, and use this expression to define the notion of a sense-datum. It is not enough that *some* ways of introducing sense-data should be vulnerable to his objection; it is essential that *all* should be vulnerable. Finally, it is not obvious that he is committed either to asserting or to denying any of the possibilities as regards what may be spoken of as being the vehicle of implication, so I shall not at the moment pursue this matter, though I shall suggest later that he can only maintain his position by giving what in fact is certainly a wrong answer to this question.

It is now time for the attack to begin. It seems to me that the contention that the fulfilment of the D-or-D condition is a necessary condition of the truth or falsity of an L-statement cannot be upheld (at any rate in its natural interpretation). For an L-statement can certainly be false, even if the D-or-D condition is unfulfilled. Suppose that I am confronted in normal daylight by a perfectly normal pillar-box; suppose further that I am in the presence of a normal, unsceptical companion; both he and I know perfectly well that the pillar-box is red. However, unknown to him, I suffer chronically from Smith's Disease, attacks of which are not obvious to another party; these attacks involve, among other things perhaps, the peculiarity that at the time red things look some quite different colour to me. I know that I have this disease, and I am having (and know that I am having) an attack at the moment. In these circumstances I say, 'That pillar-box looks red to me'. I would suggest that here the D-or-D condition is not fulfilled; my companion would receive my remark with just that mixture of puzzlement and scorn which would please my objector; and yet when he learnt about my attack of Smith's

Disease, he would certainly think that what I had said had been false.

At this point it might perhaps be suggested that though I have succeeded in producing an example of an L-statement which would be false, I have not succeeded in producing an example of an L-statement which is false when the D-or-D condition is unfulfilled; for in fact the D-or-D condition is fulfilled. For the speaker in my little story, it might be said, *has* some reason to doubt whether the pillar-box before him is red, and this is enough to ensure the fulfilment of the condition, *even though* the speaker also has information (e.g., that this is the pillar-box he has seen every day for years, and that it hasn't been repainted and so on) which enables him entirely to discount this prima facie reason for doubt. But this will not do at all. For what is this prima facie reason for doubting whether the pillar-box really is red? If you like, it is that it looks blue to him. But this is an unnecessarily specific description of his reason; its looking blue to him only counts against its being really red because its looking blue is a way of failing to look red; there need be nothing specially important about its looking blue as distinct from looking any other colour, except red. So this rescue-attempt seems to involve supposing that one way of fulfilling the pre-condition of an L-statement's having a truth value at all, consists in its having the truth-value F, or at least in some state of affairs which entails that it has the truth-value F. But surely, that a statement should be false cannot be one way of fulfilling a pre-condition of that statement's having a truth-value; the mere fulfilment of a pre-condition of a statement's having a truth-value ought to leave it open (to be decided on other grounds) *which* truth-value it has.

Let us assume that this rear-guard action has been disposed of. Then it is tempting to argue as follows: Since the objector can no longer maintain that fulfilment of the D-or-D condition is a pre-requisite of an L-statement's having a truth-value, he will have to admit that fulfilment is *at most a partial truth*-condition albeit of a special kind (i.e., is *one* of the things which have to be the case if the statement is to be true). It cannot be the *only* truth-condition, so there must be another truth-condition; indeed we can say what this is in the light of the preceding argument; it consists in the non-fulfilment of the statement's falsity-condition or falsity-conditions (which have just been shown to be independent of the D-or-D condition); to put it less opaquely, it consists in there being nothing to make the L-statement false. But now, it may be thought, all is plain sailing for the sense-datum theorist; he can simply lay down that a sense-datum sentence is to express a truth if and only if the second truth-condition of the corresponding L-statement is fulfilled, regardless of whether its first truth condition (the D-or-D condition) is fulfilled. It will be seen that the idea behind this argument is that, once the objector has been made to withdraw the contention that the fulfilment of the D-or-D condition is a condition of an L-statement's having a truth-value, he can be forced to withdraw also the contention that the implication that the D-or-D condition is fulfilled is non-detachable; and this destroys his position.

So far so good, perhaps, but unfortunately not yet good enough. For the objector has a powerful-looking reply at his disposal. He may say: 'Once again you are covertly begging the question. You are assuming, quite without justification, that because one can, in some sense, distinguish the second truth-condition from the first, it is therefore the case that the implication of the fulfilment of the first (D-or-D) condition is detachable; that is, that there must be a way of specifying the second condition which does not carry the implication that the first condition is fulfilled. But your argument has certainly not proved this conclusion. Consider a simple parallel: it is perfectly obvious that objects which are not vermilion in colour may or may not be red; so being red is not a necessary falsity-condition of being vermilion. It is also true that being red is only a partial truth-condition of being vermilion if what this means is that to establish that something is red is not enough to establish that it is vermilion. But it does not follow (and indeed it is false) that there is any way of formulating a supplementary truth-condition for an object's being vermilion which would be free from the implication that the object in question is red. This *non sequitur* is very much the same as the one of which you are guilty; the fulfilment of the D-or-D condition may perfectly well be only a *truth*-condition of an L-statement, and only *one* of a pair of truth-conditions at that, without its being the case that the implication of its fulfilment is detachable.' He may also add the following point: 'Though the contention that the fulfilment of the D-or-D condition is a pre-condition of the truth or falsity of the corresponding L-statement cannot be upheld under the interpretation which you have given to it, it can be upheld if it is given another not unnatural interpretation. I cannot, in view of your counter-example, maintain that for an L-statement to be true, or again for it to be false, the D-or-D condition must be fulfilled. But I can maintain that the D-or-D condition's fulfilment is a condition of truth or falsity of an L-statement in the following sense, namely that if the D-or-D condition *is* fulfilled, then T and F are the two possibilities between which, on other grounds, the decision lies (i.e., N is excluded): whereas if the D-or-D condition is *not* fulfilled, then one has to decide not between these possibilities, but between the possibilities N and F (i.e., T is excluded.)'

This onslaught can I think be met, though at the cost of some modification to the line of argument against which it was directed. I think that the following reply can be made: 'There is a crucial difference between the two cases which you treat as parallel. Let us endeavour to formulate a supplementary truth-condition for the form of statement "x is vermilion"; we might suggest the condition that x has the feature which differentiates vermilion things from other red things. But to suppose that x satisfies this condition, but does not satisfy the first truth-condition, namely, that x should be red, would be to commit a logical absurdity; x cannot logically differ from red things which are not vermilion in *just* the way in which vermilion things differ from red things which are not vermilion, without being red. Consequently one cannot assert, in this case, that the second truth-condition is fulfilled without its being implied that the first is fulfilled, nor can one go on to cancel this implication. But in the case of an L-statement there is no kind of *logical* implication between the second truth-condition and the first. For one thing, if there were such a logical connexion, there would also have to be such a logical connexion between the L-statement itself and the fulfilment of the D-or-D condition; and if this were so, the implication that the D-or-D condition is fulfilled would have to be carried by *what was said or asserted* by the utterance of an L-statement. But that this is not so can be seen from the unacceptability of such an hypothetical as "If this pillar-box looks red to me, then I or someone else is, or might be, inclined to deny that it is red or to doubt whether it is red". For another thing, it is surely clear that if I were now to say "Nothing is the case which would make it false for me to say that the palm of his hand looks pink to me, though I do not mean to imply that I or anyone else is or might be inclined to deny that, or doubt whether, it is pink" this would be a perfectly intelligible remark even though it might be thought both wordy and boring. Indeed I am prepared actually to say it. Consequently, although you may be right in claiming that it has not been shown that the implication of the fulfilment of the D-or-D condition is *detachable* (and indeed it may well be non-detachable), you must be wrong in thinking that this implication is not *cancellable*. Admittedly there is at least one case in which an implication which is not logical in character is at least in a sense, non-cancellable; we found one in considering example (2) "She was poor but she was honest". But if we look a little more closely we can see that the reason why the implication here is, in a sense, not cancellable is just that it *is* detachable (by the use of "and"). More fully the reason why it would be peculiar to say "She was poor but she was honest, though I do not mean to imply that there is any contrast" is that any one who said this would have *first* gone out of his way to find a form of words which introduced the implication, and *then* would have gone to some trouble to take it out again. Why didn't he just leave it out? The upshot is, that if you say that the implication of the fulfilment of the *D*-or-*D* condition is (*a*) not logical in character and (*b*) not detachable, then you must allow that it is cancellable. And this is all that the sensedatum theorist needs.' If there is an answer to this argument, I do not at present know what it is.

I will conclude by making three auxiliary points.
(1) If I am right in thinking that my objector has gone astray, then I think I can suggest a possible explanation of his coming to make his mistake. His original resistance to attempts to distinguish between the facts stated by an *L*-statement and the fulfilment of the *D*-or-*D* condition arose I think from a feeling that if the *D*-or-*D* condition were unfulfilled there would be no facts to state; and this feeling is I suspect the result of noticing the baffling character that the utterance of an *L*-statement would have in certain circumstances. But precisely *what* circumstances? I think the sort of imaginary example the objector has in mind may be the following: I and a companion are standing in front of a pillar-box in normal daylight. Each of us has every reason to suppose that the other is perfectly normal. In these circumstances he says out of the blue 'This pillar-box looks red to me' and (it is assumed) I am not allowed to take this as a joke. So I am baffled. I do not know what to make of his utterance. But surely the reason why I am baffled is that I cannot see what communication-function he intends his utterance to fulfil; it has the form of an utterance designed to impart information, but what information could he possibly imagine would be imparted to me which I do not already possess? So of course this utterance is baffling. But what the objector may not have noticed is that if in these circumstances my companion had said not 'This pillar-box looks red to me' but 'This pillar-box is red', his utterance would have been equally baffling, if not *more* baffling. My point can be stated more generally. The

objector wants to attribute to L-statements certain special features (e.g., that of being neither T nor F in certain circumstances) which distinguish them from at least some other statements. If so, he cannot derive support for his thesis from the fact that the utterance of an L-statement would be baffling in certain circumstances, when those circumstances are such that (*mutatis mutandis*) they would make *any statement whatever* baffling. He ought to take as his examples not L-statements made about objects which both speaker and audience can see perfectly clearly, but L-statements made about objects which the speaker can see but the audience cannot. But when the examples are thus changed, his case seems much less plausible.

(2) If I am asked to indicate what it would be *right* to say about L-statements and the implications involved in these utterances, I shall answer: very much the same sort of thing as I have earlier in this paper suggested as regards disjunctive statements. I don't want to duplicate my earlier remarks, so I will deal with this very briefly. (i) The fulfilment of the relevant D-or-D condition is not a condition either of the truth *or* of the falsity of an L-statement, though if this condition is not fulfilled the utterance of the L-statement may well be extremely misleading (in its implication). (ii) Like my examples (3) and (4) above, we may speak either of the speaker or of his saying what he did say as vehicles of the implication; the second of these possibilities is important in that, if I am right about it, it leads to point (iii). (iii) The implication is not detachable in my official sense. For if the implication can be regarded as being carried by his saying that (rather than something else), e.g., his mentioning *this* fact or putative fact rather than some other fact or putative fact, then it seems clear that any other way of stating the same fact or putative fact would involve the same implication as the original way of stating the fact in question. (iv) Comparably with examples (3) and (4), the implication is detachable in the further possible non-official sense which I referred to earlier in connexion with (4); there will be *some* conditions of utterance in which the implication is no longer carried, e.g., if I am talking to my oculist about how things look to me. (v) The implication is cancellable (I need say no more about this). (vi) As in the case of example (4), the reason why the implication is *standardly* carried is to be found in the operation of some such general principle as that giving preference to the making of a stronger rather than a weaker statement in the absence of a reason for not so doing. The implication therefore is not of a part of the meaning of the expression 'looks to me'. There is however here an important difference between the case of L-statements

and that of disjunctives. A disjunctive is weaker than either of its disjuncts in a straightforward logical sense, namely, it is entailed by, but does not entail, each of its disjuncts. The statement 'It looks red to me' is not, however, weaker than the statement 'It is red' in just this sense; neither statement entails the other. I think that one has, nevertheless a strong inclination to regard the first of these statements as weaker than the second; but I shall not here attempt to determine in what sense of 'weaker' this may be true.

(3) The issue with which I have been mainly concerned may be thought rather a fine point, but it is certainly not an isolated one. There are several philosophical theses or dicta which would I think need to be examined in order to see whether or not they are sufficiently parallel to the thesis which I have been discussing to be amenable to treatment of the same general kind. Examples which occur to me are the following: (1) You cannot see a *knife* as a knife, though you may see what is not a knife as a knife. (2) When Moore said he *knew* that the objects before him were human hands, he was guilty of misusing the word 'know'. (3) For an occurrence to be properly said to have a cause, it must be something abnormal or unusual. (4) For an action to be properly described as one for which the agent is responsible, it must be the sort of action for which people are condemned. (5) What is actual is not also possible. (6) What is known by me to be the case is not also believed by me to be the case. I have no doubt that there will be other candidates besides the six which I have mentioned. I must emphasize that I am not saying that all these examples *are* importantly similar to the thesis which I have been criticizing, only that, for all I know, they *may* be. To put the matter more generally, the position adopted by my objector seems to me to involve a type of manoeuvre which is characteristic of more than one contemporary mode of philosophizing. I am not condemning this kind of manoeuvre; I am merely suggesting that to embark on it without due caution is to risk collision with the facts. Before we rush ahead to exploit the linguistic nuances which we have detected, we should make sure that we are reasonably clear what sort of nuances they are.

V

I hope that I may have succeeded in disposing of what I have found to be a frequently propounded objection to the idea of explaining the notion of a sense-datum in terms of some member or members of the suggested family of locutions. Further detailed work would be needed to find the most suitable member of the family, and to select the appropriate range of uses of the favoured member when it is found; and, as I have indicated, neither of these tasks may be easy. I shall, for present purposes, assume that some range of uses of locutions of the form 'It looks (feels, etc.) to X as if' has the best chance of being found suitable. I shall furthermore assume that the safest procedure for the Causal Theorist will be to restrict the actual occurrences of the term 'sense-datum' to such classificatory labels as 'sense-datum statement' or 'sense-datum sentence'; to license the introduction of a 'sense-datum terminology' to be used for the re-expression of sentences incorporating the preferred locutions seems to me both unnecessary and dangerous. I shall myself, on behalf of the CTP, often for brevity's sake talk of sense-data or sense-impressions; but I shall hope that a more rigorous, if more cumbrous, mode of expression will always be readily available. I hope that it will now be allowed that, interpreted on the lines which I have suggested, the thesis that perceiving involves having a sense-datum (involves its being the case that some sense-datum statement or other about the percipient is true) has at least a fair chance of proving acceptable.

I turn now to the special features of the CTP. The first clause of the formulation quoted above[1] from Price's *Perception* may be interpreted as representing it to be a necessary and sufficient condition of its being the case that X perceives M that X's sense-impression should be causally dependent on some state of affairs involving M. Let us first enquire whether the suggested condition is necessary. Suppose that it looks to X as if there is a clock on the shelf; what more is required for it to be true to say that X sees a clock on the shelf? There must, one might say, actually be a clock on the shelf which is in X's field of view, before X's eyes. But this does not seem to be enough. For it is logically conceivable that there should be some method by which an expert could make it look to X as if there were a clock on the shelf on occasions when the shelf was empty: there might be some apparatus by which X's cortex could be suitably stimulated, or some technique analogous to post-hypnotic suggestion. If such treatment were applied to X on an occasion when there actually was a clock on the shelf, and if X's impressions were found to continue unchanged when the clock was removed or its position altered, then I think we should be inclined to say that X did not see the clock which was before his eyes, just because we should regard the clock as playing no part in the origination of his impression. Or, to leave the realm of fantasy, it might be that it looked to me as if there were a certain sort of pillar in a certain direction at a certain distance, and there might actually be such a pillar in that place; but if, unknown to me, there were a mirror interposed between myself and the pillar, which reflected a numerically different though similar pillar, it would certainly be incorrect to say that I saw the first pillar, and correct to say that I saw the second; and it is extremely tempting to explain this linguistic fact by saying that the first pillar was, and the second was not, causally irrelevant to the way things looked to me.

   There seems then a good case for allowing that the suggested condition is necessary; but as it stands it can hardly be sufficient. For in any particular perceptual situation there will be objects other than that which would ordinarily be regarded as being perceived, of which some state or mode of functioning is causally relevant to the occurrence of a particular sense-impression: this might be true of such objects as the percipient's eyes or the sun. So some restriction will have to be added to the analysis of perceiving which is under consideration. Price[1] suggested that use should be made of a distinction between 'standing' and 'differential' conditions: as the state of the sun and of the percipient's eyes, for example, are standing conditions in that (roughly speaking) if they were suitably altered, all the visual impressions of the percipient would be in some respect different from what they would otherwise have been; whereas the state of the perceived object is a differential condition in that a change in it would affect only some of the percipient's visual impressions, perhaps only the particular impression the causal origin of which is in question. The suggestion then is that the CTP should hold that an object is perceived if and only if some condition involving it is a differential condition of some sense-impression of the percipient. I doubt, however, whether the imposition of this restriction is adequate. Suppose that on a dark night I see, at one and the same time, a number of objects each of which is illuminated by a different torch; if one torch is tampered with, the effect on my visual impressions will be restricted, not general; the objects illuminated by the other torches will continue to look the same to me. Yet we do not want to be compelled to say that each torch is perceived in such a situation; concealed torches may illuminate. But this is the position into which the proposed revision of the CTP would force us.

   I am inclined to think that a more promising direction for the CTP to take is to formulate the required restriction in terms of the way in

[1]Op. cit., p. 70.

which a perceived object contributes towards the occurrence of the sense-impression. A conceivable course would be to introduce into the specification of the restriction some part of the specialist's account, for example to make a reference to the transmission of light-waves to the retina; but the objection to this procedure is obvious; if we are attempting to characterize the ordinary notion of perceiving, we should not explicitly introduce material of which someone who is perfectly capable of employing the ordinary notion might be ignorant. I suggest that the best procedure for the Causal Theorist is to indicate the mode of causal connexion by examples; to say that, for an object to be perceived by X, it is sufficient that it should be causally involved in the generation of some sense-impression by X in the kind of way in which, for example, when I look at my hand in a good light, my hand is causally responsible for its looking to me as if there were a hand before me, or in which . . . (and so on), *whatever that kind of way may be*; and to be enlightened on that question one must have recourse to the specialist. I see nothing absurd in the idea that a non-specialist concept should contain, so to speak, a blank space to be filled in by the specialist; that this is so, for example, in the case of the concept of seeing is perhaps indicated by the consideration that if we were in doubt about the correctness of speaking of a certain creature with peculiar sense-organs as *seeing* objects, we might well wish to hear from a specialist a comparative account of the human eye and the relevant sense-organs of the creature in question. We do not, of course, ordinarily need the specialist's contribution; for we may be in a position to say that the same kind of mechanism is involved in a plurality of cases without being in a position to say what that mechanism is.[1]

At this point an objection must be mentioned with which I shall deal only briefly, since it involves a manoeuvre of the same general kind as that which I discussed at length earlier in this paper. The CTP as I have so far expounded it, it may be said, requires that it should be linguistically correct to speak of the causes of sense-impressions which are involved in perfectly normal perceptual situations. But this is a mistake; it is quite unnatural to talk about the cause, say, of its looking to X as if there were a cat before him unless the situation is or is thought to be in some way abnormal or delusive; this being so,

---

[1] It might be thought that we need a further restriction, limiting the permissible degree of divergence between the way things appear to X and the way they actually are. But objects can be said to be seen even when they are looked at through rough thick glass or distorting spectacles, in spite of the fact that they may then be unrecognizable.

when a cause can, without speaking unnaturally, be assigned to an impression, it will always be something other than the presence of the perceived object. There is no natural use for such a sentence as 'The presence of a cat caused it to look to X as if there were a cat before him'; yet it is absolutely essential to the CTP that there should be.

In reply to this objection I will make three points. (1) If we are to deal sympathetically with the CTP we must not restrict the Causal Theorist to the verb 'cause'; we must allow him to make use of other members of the family of causal verbs or verb-phrases if he wishes. This family includes such expressions as 'accounts for', 'explains', 'is part of the explanation of', 'is partly responsible for', and it seems quite possible that some alternative formulation of the theory would escape this objection. (2) If I regard myself as being in a position to say 'There is a cat', or 'I see a cat', I naturally refrain from making the weaker statement 'It looks to me as if there were a cat before me', and so, *a fortiori*, I refrain from talking about the cause of its looking to me thus. But, if I was right earlier in this paper, to have made the weaker statement would have been to have said something linguistically correct and true, even if misleading; is there then any reason against supposing that it could have been linguistically correct and true, even if pointless or misleading, to have ascribed to a particular cause the state of affairs reported in the weaker statement? (3) X is standing in a street up which an elephant is approaching; he thinks his eyes must be deceiving him. Knowing this, I could quite naturally say to X, 'The fact that it looks to you as if there is an elephant approaching is accounted for by the fact that an elephant is approaching, not by your having become deranged'. To say the same thing to one's neighbour at the circus would surely be to say something which is true, though it might be regarded as provocative.

I have extracted from the first clause of the initial formulation of the CTP an outline of a causal analysis of perceiving which is, I hope, at least not obviously unacceptable. I have of course considered the suggested analysis only in relation to seeing; a more careful discussion would have to pay attention to non-visual perception; and even within the field of visual perception the suggested analysis might well be unsuitable for some uses of the word 'see', which would require a stronger condition than that proposed by the theory.

VI

Is the CTP, as so far expounded, open to the charge that it represents material objects as being in principle unobservable, and in consequence leads to scepticism about the material world? I have some difficulty in understanding the precise nature of the accusation, in that it is by no means obvious what, in this context, is meant by 'unobservable'.

(1) It would be not unnatural to take 'unobservable' to mean 'incapable of being perceived'. Now it may be the case that one could, without being guilty of inconsistency, combine the acceptance of the causal analysis of perceiving with the view that material objects cannot in principle be perceived, if one were prepared to maintain that it is in principle impossible for material objects to cause sense-impressions but that this impossibility has escaped the notice of common sense. This position, even if internally consistent, would seem to be open to grave objection. But even if the proposition that material objects cannot be perceived is consistent with the causal analysis of perceiving, it certainly does not appear to be a consequence of the latter; and the exposition of the CTP has so far been confined to the propounding of a causal analysis of perceiving.

(2) The critic might be equating 'unobservable' with 'not directly observable'; and to say that material objects are not directly observable might in turn be interpreted as saying that statements about material objects lack that immunity from factual mistake which is (or is supposed to be) possessed by at least some sense-datum statements. But if 'unobservable' is thus interpreted, it seems to be *true* that material objects are unobservable, and the recognition of this truth could hardly be regarded as a matter for reproach.

(3) 'Observation' may be contrasted with 'inference' as a source of knowledge and so the critic's claim may be that the CTP asserts or implies that the existence of particular material objects can only be a matter of inference. But in the first place, it is not established that the acceptance of the causal analysis of perceiving commits one to the view that the existence of particular material objects is necessarily a matter of inference (though this view is explicitly asserted by the second clause of Price's initial formulation of the CTP); and secondly, many of the critics have been Phenomenalists, who would themselves be prepared to allow that the existence of particular material objects is, in some sense, a matter of inference. And if the complaint is that the CTP does not represent the inference as being of the right kind, then it looks as if the critic might in effect be complaining that the Causal Theorist is not a Phenomenalist. Apart from the fact that the criticism under discussion could now be made

only by someone who not only accepted Phenomenalism but also regarded it as the only means of deliverance from scepticism, it is by no means clear that to accept a causal analysis of perceiving is to debar oneself from accepting Phenomenalism; there seems to be no patent absurdity in the idea that one could, as a first stage, offer a causal analysis of 'X perceives M', and then re-express the result in phenomenalist terms. If the CTP is to be (as it is often regarded as being) a rival to Phenomenalism, the opposition may well have to spring from the second clause of the initial formulation of the theory.

There is a further possibility of interpretation, related to the previous one. If someone has seen a speck on the horizon which is in fact a battleship, we should in some contexts be willing to say that he has seen a battleship; but we should not, I think, be willing to say that he has observed a battleship unless he has recognized what he has seen as a battleship. The criticism levelled at the CTP may then be that it asserts or entails the impossibility in principle of *knowing*, or even of being reasonably assured, that one is perceiving a particular material object, even if one is in fact perceiving it. At this point we must direct our attention to the second clause of the initial formulation of the CTP, which asserted that 'perceptual consciousness is fundamentally an inference from effect to cause'. I shall assume (I hope not unreasonably) that the essence of the view here being advanced is that anyone who claims to perceive a particular material object M may legitimately be asked to justify his claim; and that the only way to meet this demand, in the most fundamental type of case, is to produce an acceptable argument to the effect that the existence of M is required, or is probably required, in order that the claimant's current sense-impressions should be adequately accounted for. A detailed exposition of the CTP may supplement this clause by supplying general principles which, by assuring us of correspondences between causes and effects, are supposed to make possible the production of satisfactory arguments of the required kind.

It is clear that, if the Causal Theorist proceeds on the lines which I have just indicated, he cannot possibly be accused of having *asserted* that material objects are unobservable in the sense under consideration; for he has gone to some trouble in an attempt to show how we may be reasonably assured of the existence of particular material objects. But it may be argued that (in what is perhaps a somewhat special sense of 'consequence') it is an unwanted consequence of the CTP that material objects are unobservable: for if we accept the contentions of the CTP (1) that perceiving is to be analysed in causal terms, (2) that knowledge about perceived objects depends on causal inference, and (3) that the required causal inferences will be unsound unless suitable general principles of correspondence can be provided, then we shall have to admit that knowledge about perceived objects is unobtainable: for the general principles offered, apart from being dubious both in respect of truth and in respect of status, fail to yield the conclusions for which they are designed; and more successful substitutes are not available. If this is how the criticism of the CTP is to be understood, then I shall not challenge it, though I must confess to being in some doubt whether this is what actual critics have really meant. My comment on the criticism is now that it is unsympathetic in a way that is philosophically important.

There seem to me to be two possible ways of looking at the CTP. One is to suppose an initial situation in which it is recognized that, while appearance is ultimately the only guide to reality, what appears to be the case cannot be assumed to correspond with what is the case. The problem is conceived to be that of exhibiting a legitimate method of arguing from appearance to reality. The CTP is then regarded as a complex construction designed to solve this problem; and if one part of the structure collapses, the remainder ceases to be of much interest. The second way of looking at the CTP is to think of the causal analysis of perceiving as something to be judged primarily on its intrinsic merits and not merely as a part of a solution to a prior epistemological problem, and to recognize that some version of it is quite likely to be correct; the remainder of the CTP is then regarded as consisting (1) of steps which appear to be forced upon one if one accepts the causal analysis of perceiving, and which lead to a sceptical difficulty, and (2) a not very successful attempt to meet this difficulty. This way of looking at the CTP recognizes the possibility that we are confronted with a case in which the natural dialectic elicits distressing consequences (or rather apparent consequences) from true propositions. To adopt the first attitude to the exclusion of the second is both to put on one side what may well be an acceptable bit of philosophical analysis and to neglect what might be an opportunity for deriving philosophical profit from the exposure of operations of the natural dialectic. This, I suggest, is what the critics have tended to do; though, no doubt, they might plead historical justification, in that the first way of looking at the CTP may have been that of actual Causal Theorists.

It remains for me to show that the CTP can be looked upon in the second way by exhibiting a line of argument, sceptical in character, which incorporates appropriately the elements of the CTP. I offer the following example. In the fundamental type of case, a bona fide claim to perceive a particular material object M is based on sense-datum statements; it is only in virtue of the occurrence of certain sense-impressions that the claimant would regard himself as entitled to assert the existence of M. Since the causal analysis of perceiving is to be accepted, the claim to perceive M involves the claim that the presence of M causally explains the occurrence of the appropriate sense-impressions. The combination of these considerations yields the conclusion that the claimant accepts the existence of M *on the grounds that* it is required for the causal explanation of certain sense-impressions; that is, the existence of M is a matter of causal inference from the occurrence of the sense-impressions. Now a model case of causal inference would be an inference from smoke to fire; the acceptability of such an inference involves the possibility of establishing a correlation between occurrences of smoke and occurrences of fire, and this is only possible because there is a way of establishing the occurrence of a fire otherwise than by a causal inference. But there is supposed to be no way of establishing the existence of particular material objects except by a causal inference from sense-impressions; so such inferences cannot be rationally justified. The specification of principles of correspondence is of course an attempt to avert this consequence by rejecting the smoke-fire model. [If this model is rejected, recourse may be had to an assimilation of material objects to such entities as electrons, the acceptability of which is regarded as being (roughly) a matter of their utility for the purposes of explanation and prediction; but this assimilation is repugnant for the reason that material objects, after having been first contrasted, as a paradigm case of uninvented entities, with the theoretical constructs or *entia rationis* of the scientist, are then treated as being themselves *entia rationis*.]

One possible reaction to this argument is, of course, 'So much the worse for the causal analysis of perceiving'; but, as an alternative, the argument itself may be challenged, and I shall conclude by mentioning, without attempting to evaluate, some ways in which this might be done. (1) It may be argued that it is quite incorrect to describe many of my perceptual beliefs (e.g., that there is now a table in front of me) as 'inferences' of any kind, if this is to be taken to imply that it would be incumbent upon me, on demand, to justify by an argument (perhaps after acquiring further data) the contention that what appears to me to be the case actually is the case. When, in normal circumstances, it looks to me as if there were a table before me, I am entitled to say flatly that there is a table before me, and to reject any demand that I should justify my claim until specific grounds for doubting it have been indicated. It is essential to the sceptic to assume that any perceptual claim may, without preliminaries, be put on trial and that innocence, not guilt, has to be proved; but this assumption is mistaken. (2) The allegedly 'fundamental' case (which is supposed to underlie other kinds of case), in which a perceptual claim is to be establishable purely on the basis of some set of sense-datum statements, is a myth; any justification of a particular per-ceptual claim will rely on the truth of one or more further propositions about the material world (for example, about the percipient's body). To insist that the 'fundamental' case be selected for consideration is, in effect, to assume at the start that it is conceptually legitimate for me to treat as open to question all my beliefs about the material world at once; and the sceptic is not entitled to start with this assumption. (3) It might be questioned whether, given that I accept the existence of M on the evidence of certain sense-impressions and given also that I think that M is causally responsible for those sense-impressions it follows that I accept the existence of M on the *grounds that* its existence is required in order to account for the sense-impressions. (4) The use made of the smoke-fire model in the sceptical argument might be criticized on two different grounds. *First*, if the first point in this paragraph is well made, there are cases in which the existence of a perceived object is not the conclusion of a causal inference, namely those in which it cannot correctly be described as a matter of inference at all. *Secondly*, the model should never have been introduced; for whereas the proposition that fires tend to cause smoke is supposedly purely contingent, this is not in general true of propositions to the effect that the presence of a material object possessing property P tends to (or will in standard circumstances) make it look to particular persons as if there were an object possessing P. It is then an objectionable feature of the sceptical argument that it first treats non-contingent connexions as if they were contingent, and then complains that such connexions cannot be established in the manner appropriate to contingent connexions. The non-contingent character of the proposition that the presence of a red (or round) object tends to make it look to particular people as if there were something red (or round) before them does not, of course, in itself preclude the particular fact that it looks to me as if there were something red before me from being explained by the presence of a particular red object; it is a non-contingent matter that corrosive substances tend to destroy surfaces to which they are applied; but it is quite legitimate to account for a particular case of surface-damage by saying that it was caused by some corrosive substance. In each case the effect might have come about in some other way.

VII

I conclude that it is not out of the question that the following version of the CTP should be acceptable: (1) It is true that X perceives M if, and only if, some present-tense sense-datum statement is true of X which reports a state of affairs for which M, in a way to be indicated by example, is causally responsible, and (2) a claim on the part of X to perceive M, if it needs to be justified at all, is justified by showing that the existence of M is required if the circumstances reported by certain true sense-datum statements, some of which may be about persons other than X, are to be causally accounted for. Whether this twofold thesis deserves to be called a Theory of Perception I shall not presume to judge; I have already suggested that the first clause neither obviously entails nor obviously conflicts with Phenomenalism; I suspect that the same may be true of the second clause. I am conscious that my version, however close to the letter, is very far from the spirit of the original theory; but to defend the spirit as well as the letter would be beyond my powers.

2. ALAN R. WHITE

THE 'version of the causal theory of perception' which Mr. Grice puts before us is that (1) It is true that X perceives M if, and only if, some present-tense sense-datum statement is true of X which reports a state of affairs for which M, in a way to be indicated by example, is causally responsible, and (2) a claim on the part of X to perceive M, if it needs to be justified at all, is justified by showing that the existence of M is required if the circumstances reported by certain true sense-datum statements, some of which may be about persons other than X, are to be causally accounted for'. (A very similar view occurs in Chisholm, *Perceiving* (1957) ch. 10.) What are we to say of this?

I

First of all, a distinction should be drawn between (i) a version of the causal theory of perception from which it follows that what is to be 'causally accounted for' by the existence of the material object is a 'state of affairs' or 'circumstances' (reported by certain 'sense-datum statements') involved by the perception of the material object and (ii) a version of the causal theory of perception which holds that it is the perception of the material object which is to be 'causally accounted for' by the existence of the material object. It is the first version which Locke wished to defend and Berkeley and Professor H. H. Price to attack; but it is the second version which some recent writers (e.g., R. J. Hirst, *The Problems of Perception*, chapter 10, *passim*) seem to defend and it is this version which Professor Ryle has several times attacked (e.g., *Dilemmas*, chapter 7). More commonly, however, philosophers and philosophically minded scientists (compare Broad, *Perception, Physics and Reality*, chapter 4; Hirst, op. cit. pp. 133, 148–9, chapter 10 *passim*; Brain, *Mind, Perception and Science*, chs. 4–6) have used phrases which suggest that either they failed to distinguish between the two versions or they assimilated them on the assumption that a necessary part of the causal, or any other, theory of perception is the 'claim that perceiving a material object involves having or sensing a sense-datum'.

But even if the perception of a material object involves having or sensing a sense-datum, and if the having of this sense-datum is to be 'causally accounted for' by the existence of the material object perceived, it *does not follow* that the perception of the material object is itself to be 'causally accounted for' by the existence of the material object. This argument would only be valid either if it also contained a premiss that having a sense-datum in its turn 'causally accounted for' the perception of the material object or if it assumed, as Grice does, that the perception of a material object is the having of a sense-datum caused by that material object.

A causal analysis of *perception*, as opposed to '*sensing*', seems to me to have the difficulty that whereas failures can have sufficient conditions, successes can have only necessary conditions. If I am *prevented* from seeing (that is, it is made impossible for me to see), then it follows that I do not see; but if I am *enabled* to see (that is, it is made possible for me to see), then it does not follow that I do see.

II

To establish the thesis that to perceive a material object is to have, or involves having, a sense-datum which is 'causally accounted for' by the existence of the material object perceived, Mr. Grice has to show (i) that to perceive a material object involves having a sense-datum, and (ii) that such a sense-datum is to be causally accounted for by the existence of the material object. What proof does he offer for these two sub-theses? Let us look at the first sub-thesis.

(a) Despite the very long and elaborate argument in sections 2, 3 and 4 about 'sense-datum statements', I cannot find that he offers the slightest proof of the first sub-thesis. In the last sentence of Section 1, he says that he will 'proceed to consider at some length . . . the claim that perceiving a material object involves having or sensing a sense-datum'. And in the last sentence of the first paragraph of Section 5, he says that he hopes 'that it will now be allowed that . . . the thesis that perceiving involves having a sense-datum . . . has at least a fair chance of proving acceptable'. But what in fact has Grice done in the long interval between these remarks?

Having pointed out the difficulties of 'giving a satisfactory explanation of the meaning of the technical term "sense-datum"', and having proposed that it should be defined by reference to some such expressions of ordinary use as 'X looks Y to me' or 'it looks to me as if there were a . . .', he goes on to consider a possible general objection to this proposal, namely that such expressions 'carry the implication' that someone doubts or denies or might be inclined to doubt or deny that what is said to 'look so-and-so' or 'look as if it were so-and-so' really is so-and-so. The point of considering this objection to the proposed definition of a 'sense-datum expression' is that if the objection were true, then it would follow that such a definition would not permit a man to say in general that to perceive a material object involves having a sense-datum, since a remark using the proposed form of words could be true only if a man perceived a material object in circumstances where doubt or denial of its existence, or of its sensible characteristics, was appropriate. Such a definition of 'having a sense-datum' would therefore be of no use to a man who wanted to hold that perceiving a material object involves having a sense-datum even when there is no room for doubt or denial of the kind mentioned.

Now supposing that Grice has proved that the proposed phrases 'it looks as if . . .' etc. do not 'carry an implication' of doubt or denial, then he would have succeeded, as he correctly concludes in the opening sentence of section 5, 'in disposing of an objection to the idea of explaining the notion of a sense-datum in terms of' such phrases. But to have succeeded in showing that such phrases as 'it looks so-and-so . . .' are neutral as regards the truth or falsity of 'it is so-and-so' and could therefore be used by a man who wanted to say, 'If I perceive a material object, then it looks to me as if it were so-and-so' without his having to admit that there was any room for doubt or denial that it was so-and-so or that he perceived it to be so-and-so, is not to go the slightest way towards showing that a man who says, 'If I perceive a material object, then it looks to me as if it were so-and-so' is saying something true or even plausible. Even if, as some of Grice's remarks suggest, the alleged objector had held a much more extreme and non-linguistic thesis that whenever something appears to be so—however we try to describe this—there must always be room for doubt or denial that it is so, to have shown that he was wrong would still provide no evidence for the thesis that whenever we perceive such and such a material object, it must appear to have this or that characteristic. For all that a disproof of the objector's extreme thesis shows is that even when there is no room for doubt or denial that something has such and such characteristics, it *can* still

appear to have these characteristics and so *can* still be true to say—
however you say it—that it appears to have them.

This is why I say that Grice's argument in Sections 2, 3 and 4 provides not the slightest evidence for the truth of what he admits is a
claim which the causal theory of perception must necessarily make,
namely that 'perceiving a material object involves having or sensing
a sense-datum'. I want to make it quite clear that I am not saying
that the claim is false but only that Grice has given no evidence what-
soever for its truth.

(b) Since more than half of Grice's paper is taken up by Sections 2,
3 and 4, which contain the argument against the alleged objection
that phrases like 'it looks *A* to me', 'it looks to *X* as if it were *A*'
carry an implication that a doubt or denial that 'it is *A*' is in point,
I want to make one other criticism of his argument.

Grice says that he has 'found (this) to be a frequently propounded
objection' and maybe he could easily point to an example of it. But
as he gives no reference to any published version of this objection, I
cannot satisfy myself that he is not attributing this objection to people
who in fact hold another thesis which he himself admits to be correct.
According to Grice, those who have said that (a) such phrases as 'it
looks to me', 'it looks to me as if it were *X*' imply (b) that there is
room for doubt or denial that it is *X* have meant that such an implication is (1) carried by some of the *words* occurring in (a); (2) it is carried in
such a way that (i) any way of asserting what (a) asserts would carry this
implication (that is, the implication is 'non-detachable'); (ii) no way
of asserting (a) and (b) can be found which allows one to annul the
implication (b) without also annulling (a) (that is, the implication is
'non-cancellable'); and that (3) this implication is that (b) is a
necessary condition of the truth of (a).

Now Grice admits that (A) statements containing phrases like 'it
looks to me' do carry an implication that there is room for doubt
or denial, but the sense of this implication is that it may well be
'extremely misleading' to use such phrases when this condition is
not fulfilled. He also says that it may be 'odd or even absurd',
'prima facie odd' 'its truth might be very boring', that it has a
'*suggestio falsi*', that someone who used the phrase in this situation
'perhaps would be guilty in some sense of a misuse of *language*',
would be behaving somewhat similarly to someone who, though not
wishing to deceive and yet not believing that it is raining, nevertheless
says, 'It is raining'. I think Grice is right to stress that the remark in
question *might*, rather than *would*, be correctly judged in these ways.

For there are obvious cases where there is nothing at all wrong in saying 'X looks Y to me' where there is no room for doubt or denial that X is Y. Supposing I had read in a philosophy book that a round penny looks elliptical from such and such an angle, I might hold up a penny which I knew to be round and sadly say, 'Well, I'm afraid it still looks round to me'. Similarly, if I tried not very successfully to disguise X as Y, I might be led to say, 'It's no use, it still looks as if it were X'. Similarly, as Grice says, when telling an oculist how things look to me.

Grice also admits that (B) such a condition is implied by the speaker and/or by his saying 'it looks . . .'; and that (C) the implication is non-detachable in the sense already mentioned, though he adds that it is detachable in the sense that, though standardly carried, it is in some *circumstances*, as opposed to by some form of words, not carried. He also holds that (D) it is cancellable, that is we could sensibly use the phrase 'it looks X' and add that there is in this case no reason for doubt or denial that it is X.

It seems to follow from all this that the objection to the idea of explaining the notion of a sense-datum in terms of some variation on the phrase 'it looks to me', which Grice says is 'frequently propounded' is not that such a phrase 'implies' that there is room for doubt or denial nor that it might be 'misleading' to use it where the condition is absent, but only that it is the actual *words* of the phrases which carry some implication, that this implication is non-cancellable, and contextually non-detachable, and most importantly, that this implication which they carry is that the appropriateness of doubt or denial is a necessary condition of the *truth* of what the phrase expresses. I entirely agree with Grice that if anyone were to hold such a view, he would be mistaken. My difficulty is in finding anyone who has held this 'frequently propounded objection'. Certainly Grice has not produced anyone, nor would it be accurate to father such a view on various writers who have fairly recently suggested or said that phrases such as 'it looks . . .' commonly imply doubt or hesitation or express graded views (e.g., Ryle, 'Sensation' in *Contemporary British Philosophy*, III, pp. 434–5; Vesey, 'Seeing and Seeing As', *Proc. Arist. Soc.* LVI. (1956) pp. 109–124; Quinton, 'The Problem of Perception', *Mind*, LXIV (1955), especially pp. 31, 34; 'Seeming', Britton, Price, Quinton, *Proc. Arist. Soc., Supp. Vol.*, XXVI (1952); compare Moore, *Philosophical Papers* pp. 227–8). The nearest position I can find to that which Grice alleges to be 'frequently propounded' is contained in the following remarks by N. Malcolm ('Knowledge and Belief', *Mind*, LXI (1952) pp. 188–9). 'It would be utterly fantastic for me in my present circumstances to say "there appears to be an ink bottle here". The usage of the latter sentence would be natural only in two sorts of circumstances: either when I know or believe that there is *not* an ink bottle before me or when I am in doubt as to whether there is an ink bottle before me.' Malcolm is, of course, mistaken in saying that only in these two circumstances would it be 'natural' and not 'utterly fantastic' to use the quoted sentence, but what I want to stress against Grice is that he does not say that these two circumstances are necessary conditions of the *truth* of a statement made by the quoted sentence nor, as the context shows, does he wish to deny either that such a sentence could make a statement about 'sense-data' or that it could make it even when these two circumstances were absent.

III

I now turn to the second premiss of Mr. Grice's version of the causal theory of perception, namely, that the sense-datum which, according to the first premiss, is had when one perceives a material object is to be 'causally accounted for' by the existence of the material object.

It is important to ascertain exactly what Grice means by saying that the existence of the material object 'causally accounts for' its looking to me as if there were so-and-so, since there is nothing incompatible in denying the causal theory of perception and admitting that a reference to the material object may well 'feature in an explanation' of its looking to me as if. . . . In the middle of Section 5 he pleads, quite legitimately I think, that the causal theory be allowed to use 'members of the family of causal verbs or verb phrases'. But he then extends this plea to 'include such expressions as "accounts for" "explains", "is part of the explanation of", "is partly responsible for" '. This will not do; for anyone who attacked the causal theory would then be debarred from allowing any reference to what is perceived in an explanation of how things look to be. But to deny that X is the cause of Y is not—as the existence of many kinds of non-causal explanations show—to deny that an explanation of Y can or must contain some reference to X.

If we suppose that it is sometimes true that someone sees (or in any way perceives) a particular material object X, e.g., the word 'gaol', a snake, and also true that it looks to him as if there were a . . . , then, whether or not we also suppose as Grice does that the latter truth follows from the former, there appear to be two possibilities. *Either* it looks to him as if there were an X (e.g., the word 'gaol', a snake) *or* it looks to him as if there were something other than X (e.g., the word 'gaol', a stick). According to Grice's version of the causal theory it follows that it is true in each of these cases that the existence of the material object X (e.g., the word 'gaol', the snake) 'causally accounts for' its looking to him as if there were a . . . . . Much of what Grice says suggests that he is more interested in the case where when someone sees an X it looks to him as if there were an X, but he realizes that his theory must also cover the other case, namely when it looks to him as if there were a Y.

I argue against this that when someone sees an X and it looks to him as if there were an X, then the existence of X does furnish an explanation, though not of course a complete explanation, of its looking to him as if there were an X but it does *not* furnish a *causal* explanation; and that when someone sees an X and it looks to him as if there were something other than an X, then this has a *causal* explanation, though it also is not a complete explanation, but that it is *not* furnished by the existence of X. I presuppose that nothing said by either Grice or myself asserts or denies any facts of physiology e.g., anything about matter, waves, nerves, brain cells, etc., and their causal or other relationships.

Despite the logical differences which I shall emphasize between the two cases, there is an important similarity which I think is the root of Grice's mistakes. When it looks to me either as if *there* were an X or as if *there* were something other than an X, and it is also true that I do in fact see an X, then it follows that *something* looks to me as if *it* were an X or as if *it* were something other than an X and this something *is* X itself. Conversely, if it is true that *something* looks to me either as if it were an X or as if it were other than an X and this something *is* X itself, then it follows that I do in fact see an X. This is *not* to say that the 'it' in 'it looks as if there were . . .' and the second 'it' in 'it looks as if it were . . .' are the same. *Nor* is it to say that the person who says 'it looks as if there were . . .' must be in a position to say 'it looks as if (namely . . .) were . . .'. *Nor* is it to say that 'it looks as if *it* were . . .' follows from 'it looks as if *there* were . . .' in perceptual cases in which I do *not* see a material object or in non-perceptual cases (e.g., 'it looks as if there were some misunderstanding').

In the sense of the previous paragraph, the existence of X and the fact that it looks to me as if there were an X or as if there were other than an X provide the necessary and sufficient conditions of my seeing an X. This thesis, of course, has nothing to do with the causal theory of perception; but it may be its similarity to the thesis about necessary and sufficient conditions which Grice proposes that has, as I think, led him astray. Again, if I see an X, then whether it looks to me as if there were an X or as if there were a Y, then we may say that the X which I see either looks like an X or looks like a Y. There are reasons why an X should sometimes look an X and why it should sometimes look like a Y; the former reasons include a reference to X but they are not causal; the latter reasons are causal but include no reference to X.

It is worth noting that when a person is in the position where his sole evidence about a perceptual object is that it looks to him as if there were a . . . , then our two cases serve to differentiate two uses of 'see'. In one use a man can be said to see X, although, because it looks to him as if there were a Y, he does not realize or think that he sees X nor does he claim to see X (compare 'It was my brother not me you saw from the window'). In the other use, because it looks to him as if there were an X, he does realize or think that he sees X and claims to see X. So a person can be said to see a snake both when it looks to him as if there were a snake and when it looks to him as if there were a stick, provided that it is a snake which looks to him in either of these two ways. In the second, but not the first, use he can be said to *see that* it is an X (compare Warnock, 'Seeing' *Proc. Arist. Soc.* LV (1955)).

(i) Let us take first the case of a man who sees an X, e.g., the word 'gaol' (a snake, a bush), and it looks to him as if there were the word 'gaol' (a snake, a bush). My contention is that Grice has confused the correct point that it is, e.g., the word 'gaol' (a snake, a bush) which looks to him as if it were, e.g., the word 'gaol' (a snake, a bush) with the incorrect view that e.g., the word 'gaol' *causes, causally accounts for* etc. its looking to him as if there were e.g., the word 'gaol' (a snake, a bush). In view of something which Grice says in Section 5, I want to emphasize that in saying that his view is incorrect I do not mean that it would be 'unnatural' to say that the word 'gaol' causes it to look to me as if there were the word 'gaol', but that it would be false to say it. I want to hold that the *explanation* of its looking to him as if there were, e.g., the word 'gaol' (a snake, a bush) *when* he sees e.g., the word 'gaol' (a snake, a bush) is that he sees what he sees in normal conditions and it is an analytically true statement that the word 'gaol' (a snake, a bush) looks to normal persons in normal conditions as if it were e.g., the word 'gaol' (a snake, a bush). If X can look to anyone as if it were an X, then having a characteristic appearance is, I think, part of its being what it is. To ask someone to

point to an example of the word 'gaol' is to ask him to point to
something that, amongst other things, looks like this, viz., 'gaol'.
To say, as we may, that it looks as if it were the word 'gaol' *because*
it is the word 'gaol' is not to say that the word 'gaol' 'causally
accounts for' its looking like this, but is to explain it by reference
to the above analytical truth. *What* you see cannot be the *cause* of its
looking to you as if there were *what* you see.

I think that Grice partly sees this point at the end of the last
paragraph of Section 7, where he rightly insists that 'the non-contingent character of the proposition that the presence of a red (or round)
object tends to make it look to particular people as if there were
something red (or round) before them does not, of course, in itself
preclude the particular fact that it looks to me as if there were
something red before me from being *explained* by the presence of a
particular red object' (my italics) rather than by something else,
e.g., a trick of light. In the next clause, however, he interprets
this view, as consistency with the causal theory demands, to mean
that the explanation is of a *causal* kind. But no inference about the
type of explanation can be legitimately drawn here. For example, it
does not follow from the fact that the non-contingent truth that
irritable people tend to outbursts of anger allows us to explain a
particular exhibition of anger (as opposed to explaining it in some
other way) that, therefore, the explanation is causal. Again, we may
use the non-contingent statement that persons under eighteen cannot
be legally hanged to explain why a particular person was not legally
hanged (as opposed to explaining it by saying that he killed a man
in self-defence) without concluding that this explanation is of the
same kind as either of the other two. Grice's view that the explanation
of its here and now looking to me as if there were the word 'gaol' in
terms of the presence of the word 'gaol' is of a causal kind would
only follow if the non-contingent statement that its looking to a normal
person as if there were an X is in normal conditions due to the presence
of an X expresses a causal law. But, though I am not clear about this,
I am inclined to say that no statement of a causal law can be non-
contingent. Further, is it not the case that, *if* the circumstances are
normal, then not only does X look as if it were X but also it looks as
if there were an X then there is an X? Let me repeat that I am not
asserting or denying anything about the scientific reasons why, e.g.,
some roses look yellow and some look pink; all I am contending is
that to say that this is 'because' some *are* yellow and some *are* pink
is not to give a causal explanation, whereas to say that this is because

the sunlight is playing on them in a peculiar way is to give a causal explanation; though not one in terms of the roses themselves.

Similarly, if I murder someone I may make it look to most people as if there were an accident, or their natural ignorance may be the cause of its looking like this to them. But though an accident itself may look either as if it were an accident or as if it were murder, the accident itself does not *make* it look to anyone as if there were either an accident or a murder.

(ii) Let us turn now to the case where someone can be said to see an X, e.g., the word 'gaol' (a snake, a bush) but it looks to him as if there were something other than X, e.g., the word 'goal' (a stick, a dog). Notice that in such a case a person does not normally think or realize or claim that he sees what we say he has seen. I want to insist that it follows that *what* he sees, that is X, e.g., the word 'gaol' (a snake, a bush) looks to him as if it were a . . . , and also that it is true that there is a *causal* explanation of its looking to him as if there were a . . . , but nevertheless that the existence of the X, e.g., the word 'gaol' (a snake, a bush) does not 'causally account for' its looking to him as if there were a . . . .

Suppose that someone is reading a passage in a book; he comes across the word 'gaol', but it looks to him as if there were the word 'goal'. What sort of causal explanations would we give of this? Well, we might say that the two words are rather similar, that the printing is rather poor, that the right word in the passage would have been 'goal', that the reader was in a hurry or inattentive or poor at English, or that for some reason he wanted or expected the word to be 'goal'. But surely we could not say that the cause of its looking to him as if there were the word 'goal' was the presence or the existence of the word 'gaol'. In a more extreme case the reader might have seen in a passage the usual space between words such as in 'to have done' but read it as 'to have *been* done'. Are we to say that its looking to him as if there were the word 'been' is to be 'causally accounted for' by the presence of this normal space between words? In fact our explanations—in terms of expectation, carelessness, etc.—would make no reference to such an empty space.

More commonly than not, if it looks to someone as if there were a Y when in fact what he has seen is an X, he is deceived. As we say, he 'took' or 'mistook' the X for a Y, e.g., he 'misread' the word 'gaol' as 'goal', the typist thought I said 'and the fanatics' when I said 'mathematics'. If you '(mis)take' X for Y, then the existence of X is logically necessary to this mistake; but this is quite different from saying that the existence of X 'causally accounts for' the mistake. The causal explanation of the mistake is provided, as we saw, by reference to the condition of the percipient or the circumstances in which the mistake was made. We may say that *what* you see, the object of sight, is never the *cause* of its looking to you as if there were something other than what you see, and, contrariwise, anything that could be such a cause, e.g., a trick of light, inattention, the similarity of one object to another, is never *what* you see, the object of sight.

Again, if we allow that when someone sees X and it looks to him as if there were a Y, then he can be described as 'seeing X as a Y', my contention is that Grice has confused the correct view that it is X which is seen as a Y with the incorrect view that the presence of X 'causally accounts for' its being seen as a Y.

An interesting type of case is provided by ambiguous figures, puzzle pictures and Rorschach blots. Suppose I see the well known zig-zag line, it might look to me as if there were a zig-zag line or as if there were a set of steps or as if there were a cornice. On all three occasions, it is true that it is a zig-zag line *which* looks like this or like that, but it is *not* the *cause* of its looking like this or like that. Again, if I see a puzzle picture, it may look to me as if there were a meaningless scribble of lines or as if there were a spreading tree or as if there were a motor-cyclist upside down. The puzzle picture is the object of the various interpretations, it is *that which* is interpreted, but it is not any part of the cause of the various interpretations. Finally, when the subject looks at a Rorschach blot, there is almost no limit to what it may look to him as if there were, to what, as he says, he 'sees'. But the blot which he sees in these various ways does not 'causally account for' his seeing it in such ways.

IV

Beyond saying that phrases such as 'it looks to me as if there were a . . .' are 'sense-datum statements' and 'report a state of affairs' (or 'circumstances'), Grice does not venture any analysis of their meaning. He is, however, committed by his causal theory to the position that what such phrases signify is of such a kind that it makes sense to ask for its cause. In my objections hitherto I have assumed that this is at least sometimes true. But there is an interpretation of such phrases as 'it looks to me . . .', which many recent philosophers (e.g., Price, Quinton, Ryle, Chisholm, Smart) agree to be *one* of its ordinary meanings and some philosophers (e.g., Britton, Wittgenstein) *seem* inclined to hold is its *only* ordinary meaning. Two questions which completely bamboozle me about this interpretation are (1) Is this the *only* ordinary meaning of such phrases? (b) Whether it is or not, is this a meaning in which a request for the *cause* of its looking to me ... makes no sense? All I can do in my present shortage of space and of ideas is to make a few relevant points.

On this interpretation, 'It looks to me as if there were an *X*' and other such phrases express and, perhaps, report an inclination on my part to think that there is an *X*. To say that someone is inclined to think that there is an *X* is not incompatible with his not actually thinking there is an *X* any more than his being inclined to throw up the sponge is incompatible with his not throwing it up. Indeed, being inclined to think that there is an *X* is not incompatible with being inclined to think or with actually thinking there is a *Y*; sometimes a person cannot help thinking something to be so even when he knows that it is not so. Of course, normally, though by no means always, a person who is inclined to think that there is an *X* is not yet in a position to know whether there is an *X* or not.

This seems to be the meaning of such phrases as 'it looks to me ...' when they are employed, as they commonly are, in non-perceptual circumstances; that is, when we say such things as, 'It looks to me as if I have gone wrong somewhere, as if it is hopeless to try again, as if there were a conspiracy against me, as if we are in for an unpleasant surprise', etc. Now can we in such cases properly speak of the 'causes' of its looking to me as if ... ? Certainly, there may be *grounds* or *reasons* for my being inclined to think these things; I may be asked *why* I am inclined to think it. But the answer to this question 'why are you inclined to think that there is an *X*?' cannot properly be 'Because there is an *X*'. The reasons for thinking there is an *X* may be compelling or irresistible; I may be asked what *makes* me think or inclined to think it. But I am unhappy about saying that there may be 'causes' of my inclination to think that there is an *X*, and still more unhappy about saying that such a 'cause' could be that there is an *X*.

I also do not know how to show, or whether it is true, that the interpretation of 'it looks to me as ...' in terms of an inclination to think that ... is the *only* proper interpretation in perceptual situations; that is, in situations where we say such things as 'it looks to me as if it is bent', 'it looks to me as if there were the word "gaol", a snake, a bush'. I think I can answer certain objections which have been raised to this view (e.g., by Price in 'Seeming' *Proc. Arist. Soc., Supp. Vol.* XXVI (1952)). First, the examples of 'it looks as if ...'

already given show, I think, that this interpretation does not gain its plausibility from using 'it seems' rather than 'it looks'. Secondly, the objection that a person who *knows* e.g., that the stick in water is straight cannot mean by 'It looks to me as if it were bent' that he is inclined to think that it is bent is answered by insisting, as I did earlier, that there is no incompatibility between knowing that it is X and being inclined to think that, or indeed being unable to help thinking that, it is not X. The well known perceptual illusion tricks of psychologists are matched by the intellectual illusion tricks of sophists. Thirdly, it is objected that it is plausible to say that 'I see X' consists in nothing else but 'X's looking to me to have such and such characteristics' whereas it is 'extraordinary' to say that 'I see X' consists in nothing but an inclination to think that X has such and such visual characteristics. But the second statement does not seem to me more extraordinary than the first, especially when it is put as the view that seeing X implies that I am inclined to think that what is before my eyes is X and it is X. Would it be extraordinary to analyse 'knowing that X is Y' in terms of being inclined to think that X is Y when X is Y and being in a position to know? Of course, when it literally 'looks (or, alternatively, sounds or smells) as if', then it is normally as a result of using my eyes (ears, nose), as opposed to just 'using my brains', that I am inclined to think this. As we say, 'to look at (to listen to) him, anyone would think . . .'. Though visual hallucinations etc. suggest that it is sufficient that what I am inclined to think is that something should have visual (auditory etc.) properties. Contrast this with 'hallucinations of grandeur, of persecution' where I am inclined to think that I am God, that people are after me. Fourthly, the objection that to report what I am inclined to think is to report an unfulfilled conditional whereas to report how it looks to me is to report an actual experience is based on a confusion of the sense of 'inclined to do' which refers to what I frequently do in certain circumstances and the quite different sense of 'inclined to do' which does report an experience, something I can feel (compare White, 'Inclination', *Analysis* 21).

The strongest objection I know (e.g., Quinton, 'Seeming', *Proc. Arist. Soc., Supp. Vol.* XXVI (1952) pp. 238–9; 'The Problem of Perception', *Mind*, LXIV pp. 33–4) to confining the interpretation of 'it looks' in perceptual situations exclusively to an inclination to think is this. It is contended that when 'it looks to me' means 'I am inclined to think' as in 'It looks as if everyone is gone', statable evidence can be brought forward in support of the statement;

but no such evidence is possible for such statements as 'It looks to
me as if the stick is bent, as if the platform is moving'; therefore
the latter is not paraphrasable in terms of an inclination to think.

The answer to this objection, I think, is that, first, it is not contended
that evidence is *always* impossible whenever 'it looks as if . . .' is
used in perceptual situations; if I say, after using my field glasses, 'It
looks to me as if there is a column of troops on the horizon', I may
well be able to supply evidence. Secondly, *sometimes* no evidence or
reasons are possible for my inclinations to think so and so in non-
perceptual situations. If I ask a pupil why he is inclined to think
that every event has a cause, that the world had a beginning, that our
thoughts must exist somewhere, that the whole is bigger than any of
its parts, he might be unable to provide any reason; he might say 'It's
just obvious'. And his point might be a legitimate logical one, not
psychological. Hence I am not convinced that the possibility of there
being statable evidence distinguishes an interpretation of 'it looks . . .'
in terms of an inclination to think from some other interpretations.

But having said all this, I have to confess that when faced with
the interpretation of 'it looks to me . . .', which is almost universally
assumed, namely, that this phrase is also used for the 'description of
appearances', for the expression of 'sense-datum statements',
then I am inclined to think that (it looks to me as if) this universal
interpretation is correct.

V

SEEKING, SCRUTINIZING AND SEEING

F. N. Sibley

THIS PAPER has several connected aims. In the first place, I attempt to examine in some detail certain aspects of the logic of various perception and observation concepts, and to show some of the connexions between them. To that extent I am exploring the nature of looking, seeing, scrutinizing, etc. In order to do this I begin from some distinctions drawn by Professor Ryle in *The Concept of Mind*;[1] and I try to show both that Ryle overlooks many of the complexities of perception and observation verbs and that, as a result, he classifies some of the functions they perform in the wrong logical categories. More important, this enables us to see that what he says about seeing and the verb 'see' is either incomplete or mistaken; and it thereby clears the way for saying some positive things about the nature of seeing.

Seeking and Scrutinizing

1. Within the general category of Occurrences or Episodes, Ryle draws attention to two particularly important types of episodes which he calls, respectively, 'tasks' and 'achievements'. He claims that certain verbs and verbal expressions connected with perception, e.g. 'see', 'feel', 'look', 'listen', 'observe', 'probe', 'keep in sight', etc., fall into one or other of the two groups which he labels 'task verbs' and 'achievement verbs'. As instances exemplifying this contrast he offers the pairs 'hunting and finding', 'travelling and arriving', 'looking and seeing', 'listening and hearing' (149); and the suggestion is, here as elsewhere in the book, that there are, in each pair, not two activities, but one activity with a certain upshot or culmination. Each

From *Mind*, Vol. 64 (1955), pp. 455–78. Reprinted by permission of the author and the Editor of *Mind*.

[1] Page references are given in parentheses in the text.

pair contains a task verb and an appropriate culmination verb. Other
examples given of task words are 'scan' and 'search' (238), and, of
achievement words, 'perceive', 'detect', 'cure', 'solve', and 'hit the
bull's eye' (238). Some verbs, like 'observe' (237), 'taste' and 'smell',
may be used either as task or as achievement verbs. In this paper I
shall be interested primarily in those perception and observation
verbs which are concerned with sight, e. g. 'see', 'watch', 'gaze', 'spot',
'discern', 'notice', 'examine', 'scrutinize', 'glimpse' and 'scan',
though much of what I shall say has some application to hearing and
the other senses.

Now I think that by classifying the verbs I have mentioned as
signifying either tasks or their corresponding achievements, Ryle has
masked, misrepresented, or failed to notice some quite important
differences. One of the results of this is that he is able to conclude,
mistakenly, that the verbs 'see' and 'hear' are mainly or primarily
achievement verbs and that, as such, they stand not for activities but
for outcomes of activities. To discuss these questions, therefore, I
shall drop some of Ryle's labels and introduce some of my own.

If we confine ourselves to thinking about the sort of tasks that
may culminate in a success or a failure, and if we take, as typical
examples, racing (with or without winning) and hunting or seeking
(with or without finding), it certainly seems as if looking (contrasted
with seeing) and listening (contrasted with hearing) do fall into this
category; but it is very doubtful whether most of Ryle's other examples
do. This can be brought out by drawing attention to the contrast
between the typical use of 'look for', 'listen for', 'watch for' and
'search for', which I shall call 'seek verbs' or 'quest verbs', and that
of 'look at', 'listen to', 'watch' and 'search', which I shall call 'watch
verbs' or 'scrutiny verbs'. 'Looking for a needle in a haystack' certainly
contains a seek verb. Such looking may or may not be successful. If
it is, it terminates in finding, or seeing, or spotting, or discovering
the needle. Thus Ryle's examples, looking and listening, certainly
can be examples of activities, the successful culminations of which
are seeing, hearing and the rest. But the verbs 'look' and 'listen'
strike us as good examples of seek or quest verbs only so long as we
think of them as meaning 'look for' and 'listen for', which is exactly
what we are led to do by their occurrence in the quoted pairs 'looking
and seeing' and 'listening and hearing'. If, on the other hand, we
interpret 'look' and 'listen' as 'look at' and 'listen to', the situation
is very different. 'Looking at' is not 'looking for' and 'watching' is
not 'watching for'. The fact is, in their dominant sense, 'look at',

'watch' and 'listen to' are not quest verbs at all; nor are Ryle's other examples, verbs like 'probe', 'scan', 'savour', 'observe', examine' and 'scrutinize'. I shall classify all these together also as 'watch' or 'scrutiny' verbs, though without intending to suggest that there are no differences between them.

2. It is easy to understand how 'look at' and 'look for' might come to be confused, given the double role which 'look' may play. But the tendency to classify verbs like 'observe', 'savour' and 'examine' with 'look for', instead of with 'look at', or rather, the failure to see that there are two different types of concept here, is not to be explained in this way. It probably has two sources. First, both groups have many logical features in common. They are all activity or task verbs of certain kinds; for example, they can all be qualified by adverbs of effort, care and duration. Secondly, there are other features which, at first glance, they appear to have in common, but which in reality they do not share at all. Yet the logical differences between the two categories can, I think, be made quite explicit.

To begin with, looking for something precedes finding that something and, *a fortiori*, precedes examining it. When I look for a photograph of Westminster Abbey, I may succeed or I may fail, i.e. I may or may not spot or find it. But when I am looking *at* the photograph, or examining, scanning, scrutinizing or poring over it, the seeking and its success are behind me. What is more, it is not simply that a bit of seeking precedes a bit of examining; one might almost say that examining something is necessarily preceded by seeking and finding it (or if not by seeking, at least, as in the case of happy accidents, by finding). This is not quite true; it is a little too strong. What is necessarily presupposed is that, before you can examine something, you must have come to see it somehow. Sometimes we do come to see things by spotting or finding them and as a result of seeking. But on other occasions, as when I begin scrutinizing something in my field of vision that I have been able to see all along, it is too strong to say that I spotted or found it before I began scrutinizing it.[1] It was simply there and I could see it. However, with this reservation made, it can still be said that seeking an object does not logically require any prior occurrences of any sort, but that examining it must have been preceded by something, i.e. by coming to see it in some way. Thus, if anyone should wish to maintain that examining is really a kind of quest or seeking, he must admit that it is a different kind;

[1] The need for this proviso was pointed out to me by Mr. David Sachs. I am indebted to him for helpful discussion of several parts of this paper in an earlier draft.

it is a kind of seeking that presupposes something else, and that something else may itself be a seeking. But if this is so, then there are genuinely two types of concepts involved. Another way of putting the matter would be to say that the direct object of the verb 'seek' refers to something not yet found, while that of the verb 'examine' refers to something already found. You cannot seek an object if it is already found, or examine it before it is found.

There are other differences too. Scrutinies have no typical corresponding successes (or failures) in the way quests have. Looking for necessarily has an aim, for 'looking for' means 'trying to find'; watching need not have any aim. When I am engaged in examining the photograph, the quest for it is behind me and I am not necessarily engaged in any further quest. I can look at, scrutinize, or examine it without trying to find something. Similarly, it is quite possible to examine, say, someone's face or a painting without examining it *for* anything, that is, without seeking to find anything; you may just be trying to impress it on your memory or recording what its features are like. As a result, 'successfully', which may always apply to a quest verb, often cannot be applied to watchings and scrutinies at all. For example, 'I listened carefully for the sound of the door opening but somehow I missed it' indicates a piece of unsuccessful listening. But 'I spent the afternoon listening to their conversation' tells of neither success nor failure. It makes no sense to ask about a successful outcome to my listening; there is no outcome. Or compare the verbs in 'I went out to look for the children, saw them in the field, sat down and watched them playing'. The looking for culminated in a success, seeing or finding them, but the watching was not another bit of seeking or looking for, and met with neither success nor failure. Looking at or scrutinizing, then, are not looking for or seeking (though this is not to deny that sometimes we scrutinize in order to find); nor are all task verbs quest or seek verbs.

3. It might be thought that this is to exaggerate the difference between quest verbs and scrutiny verbs, or even to invent a distinction where really there is none. For there are, as I have said, several reasons for supposing them identical and hence for denying the distinction. I shall consider these reasons one by one.

(*a*) It is true of course, and this might seem to constitute one objection to what I have said, that sometimes, perhaps even usually, we look at, scrutinize, probe or scan with a special aim, to find something or other quite specific. Indeed, it might be urged, we seldom undertake examinations except to find something particular. Examinations are *for* something; so the expression to discuss is 'examine X *for* Y'. Moreover, when this is the case, our examinations, like our quests, sometimes succeed in discovering and sometimes fail to discover what we set out to find. Thus it might be concluded that, both in point of having a particular aim or being *for* something, and, what is a consequence thereof, in being either successful or not, scrutinies are identical with quests, or at least sufficiently like them to be grouped with them. That being so, Ryle was justified in grouping them all together as "observational undertakings, the success of which may be in question" (222) and in talking of the "corresponding successes" of these tasks. There are, after all, no differences between 'look for', 'look at' and 'scrutinize' in respect of their 'quest' element. Examining is a kind of seeking.

In reply to this objection I want to admit, of course, that remarks like 'I listened to his speech to find out his political views' and 'the doctor examined her skin for signs of measles' are natural and common enough. In some good sense we can ask whether such listenings and examinings have been successful or not. 'I was successful' would mean that I found what I was looking for or found out what I wanted to. But even so, even if examinations were always engaged in in order to find something fairly specific—and I have already argued that they are not—there would still be notable differences between quest concepts and scrutiny concepts.

(i) In the first place, the success involved in seeking X is concerned with the same object; it is finding X. But the kind of success that attends examining X is concerned with a different object, Y. You examine the photograph to find the likeness, not to find the photograph and, conversely, if you find the bloodstains, it was not the stains you were examining, but the victim's clothes. One might borrow a term from grammar and say that successes of quests are 'internal' or 'cognate' successes. Hence, even when we are examining X for something specific, which is the kind of case where, since we are trying to find something, it is plausible to call 'examining' a quest verb, success attends on the two kinds of activity in question in different ways.

(ii) It may be urged, however, that if we are to see the resemblance between quests and scrutinies, we ought to omit reference to X and compare them with respect to the object sought (Y) in each case. But even so, if for instance we concentrate attention on the fact that examining often aims at finding something, and try to compare 'seek Y' with 'examine for Y', the differences already mentioned come to light in new ways. The verb 'examine' in the expression 'examine for', being transitive, must, as a point of grammar, take a direct as well as an indirect object; and, as a point of logic, there must always be something being examined as well as something being sought (X as well as Y). Or even if—though I do not think it is so—English grammatical usage does permit, as with some other verbs (e.g. 'he is testing for radio-activity'), that 'examine' may be used without a direct object, the logical point remains: when scrutiny-verbs are used, there must be something, whether mentioned or not, which is being scrutinized. Grammatically speaking, it must always be possible to supply a direct object. Thus, though an objector might stress the 'quest' element in 'examine for', there is an irreducible complexity present which is not to be found in simple quest verbs.

(iii) Other differences still remain too; for this extra complexity results from the fact that examining X for Y is not merely seeking Y. It is doing something else as well, *viz.* some examining of X, which is a quite different kind of activity from seeking, though one which is often a good, the best, or even the only, way of finding Y. If we are looking for signs of malnutrition in the district, the best way may be to examine the children, and if we are seeking clues to the murder, we may succeed best by examining the tool-shed. Examining is, or may be, something one may do in order to find or as a means of finding. It is a way of looking for. Seeking, on the other hand, is not a way of looking for; it is looking for. 'Why is he examining X?' can be answered by 'In order to find Y', but no one would bother to answer 'Why is he looking for Y?' by 'In order to find Y'. (We should probably even interpret this question in some other way, as, e.g. 'Why does he want to find Y?') For it is analytic that you seek Y in order to find Y; but even when examining is examining for something, the kind of success involved in finding Y is not analytically connected in this way with the activity 'examining'. 'Racing in order to win' is a pleonasm, but 'running hard in order to win' is not. Seeking and hunting have their own typical or natural or, as Ryle says, "corresponding successes", but not so examining and scrutinizing. Activities of the two different types may on occasion be harnessed together in such a way that the doing of one leads to success in the other. But 'running hard' is no more identical with 'racing' than 'using a circular saw' is with 'cutting up logs'. Thus even if we consider examining as if it were always undertaken in order to find something specific, it still obviously differs from seeking.

(b) There is also, however, a second and much more natural source of confusion between quests and scrutinies. I have argued so far that there can be scrutinies with no special aim of finding this or that, and secondly that even when scrutinies have a special aim, they are still separable and distinguishable from quests. All this may be admitted. Yet it may still very plausibly be suggested that every scrutiny, even when there is no specific aim, is necessarily and by its very nature a kind of quest. For it seems obvious that any and every scrutiny aims at and succeeds in finding out something or other. People may sometimes examine without examining for this or that particular thing; but no one ever examines without finding out or at least being able to report something, that such and such was there and such and such else was not. Indeed, this is so essentially involved in examining that if, after claiming to make an examination, a person has discovered nothing at all and is quite unable to make any report, it will be said that he did not really carry out the examination, but was at best shamming or pretending. If I am asked to examine the top of the table and afterwards cannot report that, say, it is painted, polished or unpolished, rough, smooth, dented or scratched, or indeed anything at all about it, no one will concede that I have in fact examined it. There is some truth in this objection. But there are at least two good reasons why it should not lead us to ignore or deny the differences between quests and scrutinies.

(i) It is true that anyone who has carried out an examination or a scrutiny will always be in a position to make some kind of report. But it would be unnatural and improper to refer to this as a 'success'. 'Successful examination' is an appropriate expression only when, by means of an examination, a specific thing is sought and found; it is not appropriate in the kind of case now under consideration. A doctor giving a patient a routine general examination will notice and be able to report many things, a number of them being negative reactions. We may ask him afterwards if the findings of the examination were satisfactory; but it would sound most odd to ask him 'Was it a successful examination?' It would make perfectly good sense to ask him this question, on the other hand, if he were examining the patient to discover the cause of a specific pain or disorder, for it is always intelligible and never odd to ask of a quest whether it was successful or not.

(ii) The objection under consideration draws attention to the fact that any bona fide scrutiny not only aims at but must necessarily produce some positive results or findings. But this very fact itself helps to illustrate how different scrutinizing is from seeking. Whereas any scrutiny that is in some degree careful or thorough will yield some result, a quest, no matter how careful or thorough it has been, may fail to do so. It is possible to complete the course, really race hard, and yet lose the race. It is possible to search the garden for a spade and fail to find one because there is no spade there. But these failures do not entail that you were not really racing or searching. The fact that there was no spade in the garden may explain or excuse your failure to find one, but a failure it certainly was; racing hard never guarantees a victory. So even if we allowed ourselves, somewhat unnaturally, to speak of the 'success' or 'failure' of an examination, we should be forced to admit that, whereas a thorough and careful quest may lead to either success or failure, a thorough and careful examination always entails some degree of 'success'. Total 'failure' is impossible. The sentences 'If he is not trying to find out anything at all he is not really examining' and 'If he is not trying to win (find) he is not really racing (looking)' look alike, are both true, and hint that scrutinies and quests are identical. That they are not identical can be seen by contrasting two other similar-looking sentences, 'If he did not notice or discover something he was not really examining' and 'If he did not win (find the thimble) he was not really racing (looking for it)'. The former is true but the latter is by no means necessarily true.

One further objection might be raised here against my saying that any examination will produce at least some positive findings. Clearly it is possible to examine something and yet produce reports which are quite erroneous, or which omit and leave unnoticed many things that were there to be found. The quality and extent of the results depend upon the care and thoroughness of the examination. It remains true of necessity nevertheless that, as I have said, any really thorough or careful examination turns up some positive result or other, and this is not necessarily true of seeking, no matter how careful or thorough.

The reason the two foregoing points are true can be traced back to a fundamental difference between quests and scrutinies already mentioned. Examining need not have a special aim, and anything found (or even reported as not being present), no matter what it is, constitutes a positive discovery; but there cannot be a quest without a special aim, without a specific object or objects being sought. No one is ever told to go and look for whatever is there. (When we do speak of people setting out to look for whatever they can find, for example, shipwrecked mariners on desert islands, this is really only a way of referring to something or other fairly specific which is made clear by the context, say, something edible or useful. That this is so is proved by the fact that shipwrecked mariners can draw a blank. But if they were genuinely looking for 'whatever they could find', they would always find something.) It might also be noticed that, closely connected with what has just been said, there is yet a further way of emphasizing the difference between quests and scrutinies. What is found by an examination is found in the course of the examination. What is found by a successful quest, on the other hand, is found not in the course of the quest, but at the end of it.

4. The fact that some tasks are not of the type which ends in success or failure may be allowed to draw our attention to a related side-issue. I have argued that quests end in success or failure and that scrutinies as such (i.e. when not part of a quest) do not. Successes, however, are not the only kind of ends or achievements. There are several kinds of verbs, the function of which is normally to indicate not an activity, but the ending, or manner of ending, of an activity. First, there are verbs like 'cease' and 'stop'; these tell simply that an activity has ended. Secondly, there are those like 'conclude', 'complete' and 'arrive'; these signify not merely that an activity has ended, but also that it aimed at, and reached, a terminal point of some sort. Thirdly, there are those like 'win', 'find', 'spot' and 'discover' which indicate not merely stopping, nor reaching a terminal point, but gaining a success. The three types of endings (and three corresponding types of activities) can be illustrated by the following examples: (i) 'He ran for a few yards and then stopped', (ii) 'He set out to run ten laps and completed the distance', (iii) 'He ran in the race and won'. Perhaps only the second and third types should be called 'achievements', since merely to stop is not necessarily to achieve anything. But if we do use 'achievement' to cover both the second and third types, we ought no longer to equate achievements with successes as Ryle does. He groups examples of the completion type ('travel and arrive') along with examples of the success type ('hunt and find', 'look and see') and refers to them all as 'achievements or successes'.

This failure to distinguish two types of achievements, and, what results therefrom, the employment of the two labels 'success' and 'achievement' interchangeably, may also help to facilitate the erroneous assimilation of scrutinies to quests. For it is certain that scrutinies or examinations, even when they have no special aim and are not part of a quest, can lead to or end in achievements. The fact is that we almost always have standards for the completion of scrutinies. These standards may be determined according to circumstances by routine, convention, or the nature of the subject-matter. The doctor asked to carry out a thorough general examination may complete or fail to complete the task set him. The requirements for completing it are that he shall have examined a limited number of specifiable items, circulatory system, respiratory system, alimentary and digestive system and so on, and when he has completed the task he has certainly achieved something. On other occasions, the standards for completeness may be fairly arbitrary; I may announce that I have completed an examination (and not that I have merely stopped) when I have done all I intend to do or feel like doing. Other people may dispute the satisfactoriness of my standard for what constitutes a complete examination; but in all these cases, whatever the standards are, there are some standards or other for completeness. (It might be noted, however, that standards for completeness are not the same as standards for thoroughness. An examination can be thorough as far as it goes and yet be partial or incomplete.) So anyone who has carried out or completed his examination is entitled to boast of having achieved something. But only failure to differentiate could make us suppose that such an achievement is of the 'success' type, that is to say, the type appropriate to quests.

5. The outcome of this long discussion is that quests exemplify a logical category distinct from scrutinies, even though seeking may sometimes require us to do some scrutinizing. However, as I suggested earlier, it must not be supposed that within these large categories there are no differences. The notions of inspecting, investigating, probing, analysing and testing are, in the respects so far discussed, quite enough like scrutinizing and examining to be grouped all together as 'scrutinies'. But they are all different notions, and could undoubtedly be grouped according to other cross-classifications for other purposes.

Sometimes differences between concepts within the group can best be expressed by saying that the verbs mark different specific activities of a generically similar 'scrutiny' kind. For example, inspecting teeth is not probing teeth, and examining a soldier's equipment is not inspecting it, though a kit inspection will involve a certain amount of some sort of examining. They are all distinct activities. Sometimes, again, differences within the main group of scrutinies are best brought out by noticing that certain verbs are suited only to certain objects. Teeth and tissue can be probed, but not drawers or pockets. Crimes and scandals can be investigated, but not inspected. Even 'scrutinize' and 'examine', which I have so far used interchangeably, are not quite alike; the doctor does not simply scrutinize a wound, he examines it. Sometimes even, changes in the type of object sought produce some slight change of sense in one and the same verb. Looking for signs of annoyance in a face is unlike looking for pockmarks on it; it is the kind of examination that dwells on general impressions rather than the kind that demands minute attention for each and every part.

6. Next, I shall briefly mention a kind of visual activity or occurrence, in the main very different from scrutinies, yet enough like them to justify some short comments. This kind of occurrence I shall call 'mere watchings'. 'Merely watching' or 'merely looking at' is not a task, like watching, looking at, or scrutinizing. It is not something one engages in, undertakes, sets oneself to do, or applies oneself to. Consequently, the adverbs 'carefully' and 'carelessly' are both equally out of place here. If a person is idly looking or gazing out of the window watching the cars go past or the children playing in the field, and someone asks the question 'Are you watching them carefully?' the answer will be 'No'. But neither is he watching them carelessly. This kind of watching, not being a task, makes no claim to carefulness, thoroughness, or purposefulness, and so cannot be careless or slipshod either. In these ways it is unlike the sort of watching and scrutinizing we have discussed up till now, for any scrutiny is of necessity carried out with some degree of care or lack of it. Other verbs regularly used in this non-task or 'merely watching' way are 'gaze at', 'gape at' and 'stare at'. (Note that the verbs 'watch' and 'look at', but not 'examine' and 'scrutinize', can be used in both the 'non-task' and the 'task' senses.)

The point of mentioning these non-task verbs and the notion of 'mere watching' is that, differing from scrutinies in many ways as they do, they nevertheless resemble them in at least one respect. 'Gazing at', 'merely watching', 'looking at', and 'examine' all alike take, as direct object, something which has already been found or spotted or seen; that is, both scrutinies and mere watchings follow upon and, with the reservation mentioned earlier, presuppose a prior finding or a prior seeking and finding. You cannot stare at something until you have spotted or otherwise caught sight of it. In this, even if in nothing else, they deserve to be classed with scrutinies, and contrasted with quests.

Perhaps one further minor point might be made. I said above that since the notion of care applies to tasks, all scrutinies must be in some degree either careful or careless. Yet in some contexts 'a careless examination' can sound like a self-contradiction; it can sound almost as absurd as, for example, in the opposite way, 'carefully gaping' does. This is simply because we use 'examining' and other scrutiny words in two ways. Frequently they are used in the way I have described so far, that is, without any hint whether the scrutiny was careful, painstaking and methodical, or not. But they are also sometimes used with the implication that care has been taken, and then it becomes perfectly intelligible to say 'Examining carelessly isn't really examining at all', or 'I was looking at it, but I'd hardly say I was scrutinizing it'. Incidentally, too, the same dual use occurs with quest verbs, e.g. 'Yes, he was looking about for it, but you could hardly say he was searching for it'.

7. Finally, perhaps one more note should be added about the verb 'look'. Ryle talks about 'looking' without specifying either 'looking for' or 'looking at'. Guessing from the context, I have assumed that in some places, as when he refers to 'looking and seeing', he really has 'look for' in mind, and that in others, as when he groups 'looking' along with 'observing' and 'probing', he is probably thinking of 'looking at'. I have also supposed, since he makes no explicit distinction and since it seems implicit in much that he says, that he mistakenly carries over remarks that apply to one of the two categories and assumes they are equally pertinent to the other.

Be this as it may, since the verb 'look' unqualified by either 'at' or 'for', has come under notice, it is worth adding some brief remarks about its uses. Of course, it is often used elliptically instead of 'look for' or 'look at', as in 'I'm looking at the picture. Are you looking too?' But there are several other uses where this is not so. For instance, (a) the doctor who wants to examine the back of someone's head may say 'I want you to look over there'. 'To look' here means simply 'to face', and concerns only the turn of the head. The instruction can be obeyed with eyes open or shut. (b) The oculist, examining a person's eyes from the side, may also say 'I want you to look over there'. This time, following the instruction requires the eyes to be open, though position of the head is also involved. On the other hand, provided the eyes are open, no attention is required. One may be blankly gazing, unseeing, in a brown study. (c) Sometimes we are just looking or gazing out of the window, not blankly or unseeingly, but with some degree of attention. Yet, as in the two previous cases, we might deny, if asked, that we are looking *at* anything. We might hardly know even what objects we had seen, what our gaze had rested on, without making some considerable effort to recall. But this time we would be denying it, not because, as in (b), we might have been oblivious to everything about us, but because there was no one particular object or group of objects we were giving our attention to or focusing on. This 'looking' is very close to the 'merely watching' or 'merely looking at' discussed already. They are neither of them tasks, nor can they be careful or careless, etc. But they are distinguishable; for though I am not engaged in any task when I am 'merely watching' the children outside the window, I am looking *at* them and they are the main focus of whatever degree of attention I am giving. If asked, I can certainly report, without hesitation, both that I was looking *at* something, and what it was. 'Just looking out of the window' on the other hand need not be looking *at* anything.

Achievements and Retentions

So far in this paper I have tried to show that, by not treating 'look for' and 'look at' separately, Ryle jumbles together concepts of two different types. I have further suggested that his 'achievement' category contains at least two kinds of concepts, the 'completion' kind and the 'success' kind. Once these two confusions are made, it is easy to fall into supposing that 'see', which in its achievement sense certainly may indicate the success of seeking or looking for, significes likewise the "corresponding success" of visual tasks like observing, looking at and scrutinizing. But this supposition is false, first because scrutinies have no typical successes corresponding to them in the way quests have, secondly because 'see' in its achievement sense is of the 'success', not of the 'completion' type. Hence seeing is not related to scrutinizing by the relation of success to task. However, before I go on to discuss seeing, I want to examine a further issue concerning achievements.

Ryle describes achievements as the upshots or outcomes or results of certain task performances which (except when there are lucky accidents) have preceded them. He also points out that achievements differ in kind, that "Some words of this class signify more or less sudden climaxes or dénouements; others signify more or less protracted proceedings" (149), and that these latter may last "throughout a long span of time" (149). But there is much more to be said about protracted achievements, for they are very easily confused with the quite different class of episodes which I shall call 'retentions'. In fact, I think Ryle has so confused them.

If we were to seek examples of sudden achievements in accordance with Ryle's brief description, we would look for achievements, culminations and successes which occurred at a more or less precise and ascertainable moment. 'The race was won 10.4 seconds after it started', 'He achieved his two ambitions, to be knighted and to live to his eightieth birthday' and 'His aim was to spot the first plane over the horizon, which he did at 08.53 hrs.' are all suitable examples. They are the kinds of achievements clockable with stop-watches, photo-finishes, or at least by a definite date on a calendar. On the other hand, if we look for examples of protracted achievements, we need cases where, though some rough period can be mentioned within which the success was achieved, no precise moment, whether second, minute or day, can be singled out as *the* moment of the achievement. Typical illustrations would be 'His aim was to reach a ripe old age, and he did', 'He hoped for, and found, contentment in his declining years' and 'After much effort he succeeded in reaching a place of eminence in his profession'. With these protracted and unclockable events, a moment or date may be given when the goal has certainly not yet been reached, and another when it certainly has; but it is impossible to come any closer to an exact moment within that period. There is no exact moment at which it happened.

If we were setting out to differentiate sudden from protracted achievements, these are the sorts of illustrations we would expect. However, the examples Ryle gives as instances of protracted achievements are very few, and in fact illustrate a quite different logical category. Few, if any, true examples of protracted achievements are to be found in *The Concept of Mind*. Ryle's main example is 'keeping it in view', and to this he adds that "the secret may be kept, the enemy held at bay, or the lead be retained, *throughout a long span of time*" (my italics). But these do not illustrate protracted achievements at all. They illustrate the logical category I am labelling 'retentions'.

The differences between protracted achievements and retentions can be clearly exhibited, though it is not hard to see how they come to be confused. In the first place, protracted achievements are (or may be) genuine culminations, even though unclockable ones, of tasks or activities like seeking and aiming at. Retentions, on the contrary, are not merely culminations or outcomes or typical successes of such task activities at all; as a matter of fact they are themselves tasks of a sort. This can be emphasized in several ways. Looking for the snake is one thing, finding or spotting it is the successful end of looking, and keeping it in sight is something you do *afterwards*. Similarly with 'he took the lead and kept it' or 'he acquired a high reputation in his profession and retained it till his death'.

Secondly, retentions presuppose prior achievements at least to the extent that scrutinies do (that is, with the reservations already made on page 129), and so cannot themselves be achievements, either sudden or protracted. 'He kept it in sight from ten o'clock till five minutes past' entails that, at ten o'clock or before, he either caught sight of or spotted it (sudden achievement), or else gradually made it out, discerned it in the mist, or some such thing (protracted achievement). Whether the achievement was sudden or protracted, deliberate or accidental, the retention must have been preceded by it and was distinct from it. In short, keeping a title is not itself a kind of winning; and retaining the lead is not the same as taking the lead, though whoever retains it must have taken it, whether by accident or by effort and competition. It is worthy to notice too that one can succeed, yet fail to retain, e.g. 'He tried to seize the snake, caught hold of it, but was unable to retain his hold on it even for a second'.

Thirdly, the notion of 'duration' or 'protractedness' is different in the two cases. Ryle's expression which I italicized above, 'throughout a long span of time', is ambiguous. With protracted achievements, it means that success came between such and such times or dates, even though, between those times, there was no specifiable or clockable moment at which it could be said to come. At one moment success had definitely not yet come, and by some later moment it had. This is surely implied in Ryle's contrasting account of sudden achievements as occurring "at a *specifiable* instant" (149) (my italics). But with retentions, and with Ryle's examples, a second interpretation is needed. If I keep the lead for ten minutes, the keeping or retaining is not something that comes to fruition sometime within the ten minutes but for which no exact time, other than extreme limits, can be given; it is something lasting all the while and going on the same at every moment between the two specified limits. Protracted achievements have no beginnings or endings for they are themselves, unlike retentions, protracted or drawnout endings. The fact that 'duration' and 'long-lasting' mean something different in the two cases also explains why, whereas every retention must have some, even if a very short, duration, there can be 'sudden' achievements which have no duration at all. There could not be a retention that lasted no time at all.

Fourthly, and as a result, the notion of success applies differently. It is equally true both that one cannot win, find, glimpse or attain unsuccessfully, and also that one cannot retain or keep something in sight unsuccessfully. Undoubtedly this fact, that both achievements and retentions are logically incapable of failure, has been one of the main reasons for confusing them, and it is easy to see how a label like 'protracted achievements' could be applied to both categories. But they are different even so. If a runner keeps the lead for three minutes, or if I keep my grip on the snake for thirty seconds, something is being done, some task carried out with success, at all times throughout the period; no failure occurs at any moment. Failing to retain would mean ceasing to retain; but as long as retention continues, it is all the while both a success and an activity. Holding on for dear life is no less of an activity for the fact that, while it is being done, it is always being done successfully. On the contrary, the protracted success which consists in gradually making out a form in the mist, or attaining fame or political wisdom between two limiting times or dates, is not a task or activity to which the adverb 'successfully' applies at every moment throughout the period. For attaining is not an activity at all, but the success or outcome of some kind of activity.

Fifthly, and closely connected, is the different way the notion of effort applies. Achievements, as such, and as Ryle makes plain, require no effort. They crown other effortful activities. So protracted achievements, as such, require no effort either. As long as the effort is still continuing, success has not yet been really or fully gained; and when it is gained, that effort is over. But retentions are frequently arduous and demand continued effort, not an effort aimed at a future result or culmination, but an effort to hold on to what was gained in the past.

It is clear then that protracted achievements are not retentions; but clear also why it was easy to confuse the two categories, even to the extent of giving typical retention verbs as examples of protracted achievements. (a) Both retentions and achievements may follow upon seekings; but whereas retentions are further activities that may follow, achievements are the culminations of the earlier activities. Achieving may follow upon seeking, but retaining follows both. (b) Duration, success and perhaps effort (as in the similar-looking sentences 'he made great efforts to achieve' and 'he made great efforts to retain') appear to apply equally to both concepts; but they all apply in different ways or senses. The fact is that, in spite of many apparent similarities, retention verbs form a special or distinct group of task verbs, unlike either quest verbs or scrutiny verbs in many ways, and certainly unlike any kind of achievement verb.

Seeing

1. So far, I have separated out the concepts of seeking, scrutinizing, achieving and retaining, and suggested some of the relationships which may hold between them. What follows is a partial examination of some uses of the verb 'see' (and, by implication, of other perception verbs like 'hear' as well).

A reading of some sections of *The Concept of Mind* leaves the impression that many, though not all, of the traditional problems concerned with seeing, hearing, etc., arise from mistakes about the logic of the verbs 'see' and 'hear'. It is suggested and emphasized again and again throughout the book that, whereas seeing and hearing have often been thought of as mental, private, or hidden activities or processes, they are, in reality, not activities at all, but achievements or triumphs in which activities may culminate. If they are not activities or goings-on, then, *a fortiori*, they are not hidden or private or mental goings-on. The verbs signify the moments and manners of culmination of such public and witnessable activities as looking for and listening for. There is something about this line of argument that gives temporary satisfaction, for it may well be true that 'he heard it', 'I see it' and the like are frequently used in an achievement sense. However, I think it is clear that the verbs 'see' and 'hear' are not always or exclusively used in achievement senses. They are used in a number of other ways which Ryle either overlooks or at least fails to discuss. This explains why the line of argument suggested above does not satisfy for long.

One reason for focusing too exclusively on the achievement use of 'see' has already been indicated. The confusions discussed in the first part of this paper lead smoothly to the conclusion that the role which 'see' plays in relation to observations and scrutinies is an achievement one. It is then easily supposed that the main function of 'see' in connexion with visual activities has been accounted for. It escapes notice that seeing, in this 'spotting' sense, precedes observing, and is over and done with by the time observation or scrutiny is under way. As a result, too, it easily escapes remark that, when we are observing or scrutinizing, there is another use of 'see' which is not over and done with and which needs to be accounted for. This is quite certainly not an achievement use.

The sense of 'see' I have in mind is that in which, to look at or scrutinize an object for a given length of time, one must *throughout that length of time* be seeing it. I cannot scrutinize something unless I can, at the time, actually see it (though of course I may see it without scrutinizing it). If for any period of time I am unable to see the object in question, for that length of time I cannot scrutinize or examine it. If 'he is now watching it' is true, 'he can now see it' must also be true. So here is at least one use of 'see' which is clearly different from the achievement or spotting use and which needs further discussion. (I have been prepared to grant, for the purposes of this article, that 'see' is sometimes an achievement verb. It might be questioned whether even this much is true. There may be some visual achievement verbs; perhaps 'descry', 'spot' and 'espy' are examples. But surely it would be hard to find an occasion where someone who had looked for and suddenly seen something would reject the question 'Did you see it for long?' as an absurd one. Yet strictly, if 'see' is ever an achievement verb, it should be possible to find such occasions.)

The things to notice about this non-achievement use of 'see', then, are the following. First, seeing follows upon and presupposes the prior occurrence of a spotting or seeing of either the sudden or protracted achievement kind. In this respect it is similar both to scrutinizing and to keeping in sight. Secondly, seeing, in this sense, lasts through time; duration phrases like 'for a long time' or 'for five minutes' can apply to it. So once again it is distinguished from the sudden achievement use of 'see'; and since the notion of duration which applies is, as with retention and scrutiny verbs, the notion of lasting throughout a period, it is also distinguished from protracted achievements. When we say 'he could see it uninterruptedly from 2 p.m. until 2.10 p.m.', we are saying that something began at 2 p.m. and lasted 10 minutes; we are not saying that these two times are limits within which something that cannot be any more exactly dated occurred. Thirdly, seeing is a precondition of scrutinizing and hence not itself a kind of scrutinizing. In this respect, the retention notion, 'keeping in sight', has a close affinity with seeing. You cannot scrutinize an object unless you can see it or unless you keep it in sight; so retentions also are often presupposed by scrutinies. In a number of respects then, 'seeing X' is very much like the retention, 'keeping X in sight', for they both differ from, and are related to, activities like seeking, spotting, and scrutinizing in much the same way.

Despite these many similarities, however, seeing is certainly not to be classified as a 'retention'. Though seeing and keeping in sight are similarly related to scrutinies, they are not identically related; for whereas it is often, but not always, the case that one has to keep an object in sight in order to be able to scrutinize it, it is without exception always the case that one must be able to *see* an object in order to scrutinize it. This shift from 'often' to 'always' is an indication of an important difference. Someone chasing a rabbit or a mosquito, or watching the activities and movements of an ant in the grass or a plane in the distance, must manage, if he is to continue to watch or otherwise scrutinize the object, to keep it in sight. These are all cases where effort is needed, where the object is elusive, small, retreating, or fast-moving, where the medium is fluctuating, full of obstacles, or otherwise not at its best, where, in short, there is a chance of the object hiding, or escaping, or of our losing it. But if I am examining something which is motionless and in plain view in front of me, if I spend five minutes, say, on a clear day looking carefully at the nearby mountains, it must certainly be true, for as long as I am looking at or scrutinizing them, that I can see them. Yet we would hardly say that I was keeping them in sight; they are not likely to hide or move away.

What I am suggesting, in effect, is that the main difference between 'keeping in sight' and 'seeing' is one of effort, or difficulty, or purposefulness, or task-activity. It is like the difference between keeping the lead and merely being ahead. Being ahead, having the lead, and enjoying a reputation may need no effort; they are not *doing* anything. *Keeping* ahead or *guarding* a reputation imply effort or watchfulness, and may demand strong measures. They are something one *does*. It might be said, in fact, that a retention verb like 'keep in sight' is an effort-implying or active form of the effortless (or noncommittal) 'can see' form. That this is so can be proved by the fact that we can usually paraphrase 'he kept it in sight' by, for example, 'he did what was necessary (turned his head, moved round, ran, pursued, dodged) to ensure that he might continue to see it'. This explains why, as I said, scrutinizing or looking at an object always and necessarily involves seeing the object, but only sometimes (e.g. when the object is moving or elusive) involves the effortful activity of keeping it in sight. If this is so, 'keeping it in sight' is, one might say, simply a logically more complex version of 'seeing it'; for while it includes the notion of seeing—anyone keeping the moving object in sight can, *a fortiori*, still see it—it also includes the notion of successfully doing something, unspecified, in order to continue seeing it. Hence, the logical features of the two concepts and their relations to other concepts are in part very similar, as we have noticed; but because of its extra complexity, there are additional features that apply to the one but not to the other. Keeping it in sight is a task or activity, something one does, sets oneself to, or engages in. It can be done skilfully, carefully, resolutely, doggedly, with all one's strength and with great effort and expenditure of energy. None of this is true of simply seeing something. We might almost call 'see' a verb of 'having' or 'possession' to contrast it with verbs of 'keeping' or 'retention'. About certain other verbs in another context Ryle says, "they do not directly report gettings, but something nearer akin to possession" (303). Replace 'gettings' by 'keepings', and his remark would apply to perception verbs and exactly fit the present case.

2. It will be noticed that, in illustrating this use of 'see', I have, following normal English practice, frequently used 'can see' or 'could see', rather than simply 'see' or 'saw'. Since 'can' and 'could' are often the hall-marks of potentialities, abilities, or dispositions, rather than of actual occurrences or happenings, it might be supposed or argued that what I am discussing is merely a dispositional use. One thing seems plain however. If we had to classify the use of the sentence 'he could see it clearly for ten whole minutes' by means of a simple dichotomy, we should have to choose 'occurrence' or 'happening' or 'exercise of an ability', rather than 'potentiality' or 'disposition' or 'ability'. So the use of 'can' or 'could' is not in this case (or in the case of other perception verbs like 'hear', 'smell' and 'taste') concerned merely with statements about unactualized dispositions or unexercised abilities. Indeed it seems to be a peculiarity of certain languages only, among which English is one and German another, to use 'can' or its equivalent with non-dispositional uses of perception verbs. In other languages, a simple present or past tense of the verb 'to see' seems to be either the only or the most usual way of expressing the occurrence sense. For instance, we translate 'I can still see it over there' by *'Je le vois . . .'* (not by *'Je peux le voir . . .'* which regularly connotes mere possibility); and in Spanish, although *'ver'* is sometimes used with *'poder'*, it is much more frequently used without. What is more, even in English, especially when we are emphasizing that the verb is not to be understood in a merely dispositional sense, we sometimes omit the 'can' and 'could'. The following scraps of conversation are not grammatically abnormal, and certainly do not deal only with abilities: 'Did you see it?—Yes, I saw it for about five minutes without interruption'; 'I don't believe you can see it now or that you ever have seen it.—On the contrary, I actually see it at this very moment and have been seeing it for the last two minutes'; 'I have thee not, and yet I see thee still'. However, it is not the peculiarities and modes of expression of this or that language that interest

us here; it is the kind of use to which certain expressions are put, no matter what their language, their grammatical construction, or their verbal characteristics. As the use of 'see' or 'can see' that we are considering is quite certainly not a dispositional use, its grammatical appearance need not worry us.

Two warnings are needed here. (a) When I say that the use of 'see' or 'can see' under discussion is concerned with the exercise of an ability, not merely with an ability, it must not be supposed that I am asserting that the same verbal expressions are never used in a dispositional sense. They quite obviously are used in both ways. 'We could see the sea from our window' and 'He can see the river from his house' may tell of possibilities. In many contexts it would be absurd to retort, for example, 'He can't, because he's not even in his house at the moment', or 'But he's asleep at the moment, so of course he can't'. Yet the same form of words, 'We could see the sea' and 'He can see the river', may, in another context, report a visual occurrence, and may be queried by, e.g. 'But you were looking the other way all the time', or 'But his eyes are closed'. (b) I am not saying that the dichotomy 'disposition or occurrence' is in fact exhaustive. In maintaining that the use of 'see' under discussion is not a dispositional one I am not claiming that, when someone sees, he is engaged in an 'activity', or that anything is 'going on'. Perhaps even the expression 'occurrence use' is objectionable or a misnomer. However, I shall continue to use it with the understanding that it serves to contrast this use of 'see' with the obviously dispositional use already described.

3. I argued above that the verb 'see', which I there characterized for purposes of contrast as a verb of 'possession' or 'having', cannot be qualified by adverbs of effort. Certain additional remarks ought perhaps to be made in this connexion. We often employ the verb 'see', amongst others, without any grammatical object. This happens both with the occurrence use, as in 'When I open my eyes I can see', and with the dispositional use, as in 'Of course John can see, but he's asleep at the moment' (where 'can see' has the force of 'is not blind'). In these cases the omission of a grammatical object is not a mere ellipsis by which reference to a known specific object is omitted, as in 'I want you to look at the blackboard. Can you see?' On the contrary, no object is mentioned because there is no specific object in question. The man whose cataract has been removed, when asked after the operation 'Can you see?', does not counter with 'Can I see what?' We are enquiring about his eyesight; we were not enquiring about

eyesight when we asked 'Can you see?' in the blackboard example. Thus we employ 'see' without a specified object when we are concerned with seeing for its own sake, without taking any interest in, or making any reference to, what is seen. If any grammatical object had to be supplied, it would be, depending on circumstances, an expression like 'anything', 'something or other', or 'whatever is there to be seen'.

I hesitate to say that the verb is used in different senses in the two sentences 'I can see' and 'I can see it (the blackboard, etc.)'. What is certain is that the emphasis and purpose of the two remarks would be very different; one stresses visual capacities and performances, the other the presence or the discovery of an object. Because of this, there are numerous conditions that may need to be fulfilled before you may justly claim that you can actually see some specified object or other, and, conversely, numerous reasons why you may fail to see it. You will see it 'if you turn round', 'if it is there today', 'if there are no intervening obstacles', 'if the light is good and there is no mist', 'if you are facing due south', and so on. When no specific object is in question, but only whether you can see or not, these and similar conditions are irrelevant. In particular, and this is why I introduce the issue here, making an effort or trying is something which is never relevant to seeing as such. We do of course use sentences like 'he made great efforts to see what his rival was doing' and 'he tried to see the whole procession'. But in all such cases there is a specific object involved, and the trying or resolving is concerned with getting into, or staying in, a position from which one can see that object. In trying to see the procession we may need to climb the building and crane our necks past the chimney pots or the gargoyles; there the trying ends. Once we are in position, with our eyes open, seeing is effortless, or more strictly neither effortful nor effortless. It is neither difficult nor easy; it simply occurs. So when seeing alone, and not a specific object, is in question, effort is not either appropriate or possible. Nothing is to be gained by exhorting someone to try to see; if people are awake and their eyes are open, either they see, or else they are blind from some cause and do not.

One final point. Whether or not we should think of the use of 'see' with a specific object and the use of 'see' without an object as two distinct senses of the verb, the following statements are true. Whenever it happens that I can see a particular object, say, the blackboard, it is true *a fortiori* that I can see, but the converse is not necessarily true. What is more, not only is 'I can now see' entailed by 'I can now see it' and hence also in turn by 'I am keeping it in sight' and 'I am looking at or scrutinizing it' (all of which follow upon the spotting of the object); 'I can now see' is entailed, in addition, by 'I see it' (in the spotting or achievement sense), and even by 'I am looking for or seeking it' (which occurs before the spotting of the object). Thus, the occurrence use of 'see' without a specific object underlies visual scrutinies, retentions, achievements and quests. It seems to be the most fundamental use of 'see', and is involved in all the other visual concepts already discussed.

Summary

I shall now sum up briefly. By distinguishing 'looking for' from 'looking at', we are forced to notice that perception verbs, like 'see', have other functions besides indicating achievements. Among these other functions, some at least deal with 'happenings' or 'occurrences', that is, they signify the exercise, for a period of time, of an ability, not merely the possession of an ability. Further, when the differences between retentions and protracted achievements are pointed out, we are able to see how the use of an expression like 'keeping it in sight' is related to one of these occurrence uses of 'see'. The removal of the erroneous view that perception verbs are mainly achievement verbs, and the directing of attention to their occurrence uses, clears the way for further discussion of the logic of seeing. I have in fact indicated some of the logical features of seeing and some of the relations which hold between it and other visual concepts. But much still remains to be said. In particular, the conclusion that seeing is not an activity (and hence not a mental activity), which was founded upon the contention that perception verbs are a type of achievement verbs, can no longer be upheld on those grounds. The issue, therefore, whether seeing is or is not describable as an activity needs to be reargued with reference to the occurrence uses of perception verbs. But that is not possible here.

NOTES ON THE CONTRIBUTORS

O. K. BOUWSMA has for many years been Professor of Philosophy at the University of Nebraska. He was John Locke Lecturer in Oxford in 1950, and his *Philosophical Essays* were published in 1965.

R. J. HIRST is Professor in Logic at Glasgow University. His book *The Problems of Perception* was published in 1959, and he also edited, in 1965, a collection of readings under the title *Perception and the External World*.

RICHARD WOLLHEIM is Professor of Philosophy at University College, London. His critical Study *F. H. Bradley* appeared in 1959.

ANTHONY QUINTON is a Fellow of New College, Oxford. He is the editor of *Political Philosophy* in the present series.

H. P. GRICE is a Fellow of St. John's College, Oxford, and was William James lecturer at Harvard in 1967.

ALAN R. WHITE has been Ferens Professor of Philosophy in the University of Hull since 1961. Among his publications are *G. E. Moore: A Critical Exposition* (1958) and *Attention* (1964), and he is the editor of *The Philosophy of Action* in the present series.

F. N. SIBLEY, after teaching for some years in universities in the United States, has recently been appointed Professor of Philosophy in the University of Lancaster.

BIBLIOGRAPHY

(not including material in this volume)

I. BOOKS

The following recent or fairly recent books deal wholly or in part with philosophical problems of perception.

ARMSTRONG, D. M., *Perception and the Physical World* (Routledge and Kegan Paul, London, 1961).

AUSTIN, J. L., *Sense and Sensibilia* (Clarendon Press, Oxford, 1962).

AYER, A. J., *The Foundations of Empirical Knowledge* (Macmillan, London, 1940).

AYER, A. J., *The Problem of Knowledge* (Macmillan, London, 1956). This work is also published by Penguin Books: the main discussion of perception is in *Chapter 3*.

BRAIN, Lord, *The Nature of Experience* (Oxford University Press, London, 1959).

CHISHOLM, R. M., *Perceiving: A Philosophical Study* (Cornell University Press, Ithaca, N.Y., 1957).

GARNETT, A. C., *The Perceptual Process* (Allen and Unwin, London, and University of Wisconsin Press, Madison, 1965).

HAMLYN, D. W., *The Psychology of Perception* (Routledge and Kegan Paul, London, 1956).

HAMLYN, D. W., *Sensation and Perception* (Routledge and Kegan Paul, London, 1961).

HILL, T. E., *Contemporary Theories of Knowledge* (Macmillan Company, New York, 1961).

HIRST, R. J., *The Problems of Perception* (Allen and Unwin, London, and Macmillan Company, New York, 1959).

LEAN, M., *Sense-Perception and Matter* (Routledge and Kegan Paul, London, 1953).

PRICE, H. H., *Perception* (Methuen, London, 1932).

PRICE, H. H., *Hume's Theory of the External World* (Clarendon Press, Oxford, 1940).

RYLE, G., *The Concept of Mind* (Hutchinson, London, 1949).

RYLE, G., *Dilemmas* (Cambridge University Press, Cambridge, 1954).

SMYTHIES, J. R., *Analysis of Perception* (Routledge and Kegan Paul, London, 1956).

WHITE, A. R., *G. E. Moore: A Critical Exposition* (Blackwell, Oxford, 1958).

WYBURN, G. M., PICKFORD, R. W., and HIRST, R. J., *Human Senses and Perception* (Oliver and Boyd, Edinburgh and London, 1964).

These three authors deal respectively with physiological, psychological, and philosophical problems of perception, each writing primarily for the non-specialist in his particular field.

II. ARTICLES

(1) *Theories of Perception*

AYER, A. J., 'Phenomenalism', *Proceedings of the Aristotelian Society* (1947–8).

FIRTH, R., 'Sense-data and the Percept Theory', two articles, *Mind* (1949 and 1950).

FIRTH, R., 'Phenomenalism', in *Science, Language, and Human Rights*, American Philosophical Association, Eastern Division (1952).

HIRST, R. J., 'Perception, Science, and Common Sense', *Mind* (1951).

LEWIS, C. I., 'Realism or Phenomenalism?', *Philosophical Review* (1955).

MACDONALD, Margaret, 'Linguistic Philosophy and Perception', *Philosophy* (1953).

WATLING, J., 'The Causal Theory of Perception', *Mind* (1950).

WILLIS, R., 'The Phenomenalist Theory of the World', *Mind* (1957).

(2) *Sense-data and Their Critics*

ADAMS, E. M., 'The Nature of the Sense-datum Theory', *Mind* (1958).

ALSTON, W. P. 'Is a Sense-datum Language Necessary?', *Philosophy of Science* (1957).

BARNES, W. H. F., 'The Myth of Sense-data', *Proceedings of the Aristotelian Society* (1944–5).

BARNES, W. H. F., 'On Seeing and Hearing', in *Contemporary British Philosophy*, 3rd Series, ed. H. D. Lewis (1956).

BLACK, M., 'The Language of Sense-data', in *Problems of Analysis* (1954).

BRITTON, K., Price, H. H., and Quinton, A. M., 'Seeming', *Aristotelian Society, Supplementary Volume* (1952).

BROWN, N., 'Sense-data and Material Objects', *Mind* (1957).

FIRTH, R., 'Austin and the Argument from Illusion', *Philosophical Review* (1964).

MOORE, G. E. 'Visual Sense-data', in *British Philosophy in Mid-century*, ed. Mace (1957).

PRICE, H. H., 'The Argument from Illusion', in *Contemporary British Philosophy*, 3rd Series, ed. H. D. Lewis (1956). Also in this volume:

RYLE, G., 'Sensation'.

SHWAYDER, D. S., 'The Varieties and the Objects of Visual Phenomena', *Mind* (1961).

YOLTON, J. W. 'A Defense of Sense-data', *Mind* (1948).

YOLTON, J. W., 'Linguistic and Epistemological Dualism', *Mind* (1953).

(3) *Miscellaneous*

ARMSTRONG, D. M., 'Illusions of Sense', *Australasian Journal of Philosophy* (1955).

FRÖHLICH, F., 'Primary Qualities in Physical Explanation', *Mind* (1959).

HANSON, N. R., 'On having the same Visual Experiences', *Mind* (1960).

MALCOLM, N., 'Direct Perception', *Philosophical Quarterly* (1953).

SELLARS, R. W., 'Sensations as Guides to Perceiving', *Mind* (1959).

VESEY, G. N. A., 'The Location of Bodily Sensations', *Mind* (1961).

WARNOCK, G. J., 'Seeing', *Proceedings of the Aristotelian Society* (1954–5).

INDEX OF NAMES

(not including authors mentioned only in the Bibliography)